HELLO, DEAR READER

Thank you for choosing my book, "DASH Diet Cookbook for Beginners." I hope this culinary journey will bring you immense benefits and pleasure as you work towards a healthier lifestyle through balanced nutrition.

We live in a time of constant stress, limited time for cooking, and an overwhelming selection of unhealthy foods, all of which can make this path challenging. That's why I created this book—to help you find a balance between delicious meals and healthy eating. This book reflects my experience and dedication to promoting a healthy lifestyle. My goal is to assist you on your journey. I hope this book inspires you to make positive changes and enjoy all the benefits of the DASH diet.

Best wishes,
Christopher Donovan

We hope this book becomes an invaluable tool in your journey towards a healthier lifestyle and that you enjoy every recipe! Your opinion is incredibly important to us, so we invite you to share your impressions and recommendations. Your reviews help other readers make informed decisions and help us understand what you find valuable.

To leave a review, scan the QR code below by activating the camera on your smartphone or open a QR code scanning app. Leave your review and feel free to add photos and videos. Then press 'Submit'.

US　　　　　　　　　　UK

We greatly appreciate your input and hope you enjoy your part in better health!

Christopher Donovan & the publishing team

TABLE OF CONTENTS

INTRODUCTION

What is the DASH Diet?....................................7
The Basics of the DASH Diet 7
The DASH Diet is Recommended for 8
DASH Diet & Sodium 9
Recommended Foods for the DASH Diet 10
Foods to Limit on the DASH Diet....................11
Daily Nutrient Levels in the DASH Diet 13
Daily Nutrient Guidelines for DASH..................14
How to Create Your DASH Diet Meal Plan 15
Balanced DASH Diet Meal Plan Rules................16
Blood Pressure Diary 17
30 DAY MEAL PLAN 18
DASH Diet Shopping List 21
DASH Diet and Weight Loss......................22
Recommendations for Weight Loss 23
Measurement Conversion Chart......................24
Dish Symbols Explanation......................24

BREAKFAST

Oatmeal with Fresh Berries and Nuts 26
Greek Yogurt with Honey and Walnuts...............26
Spinach and Mushroom Egg White Omelet 27
Vegetable Omelet with Herbs.............................27
Avocado and Egg Toast......................28
Cottage Cheese with Fruits and Honey 28
Muesli with Yogurt and Fresh Fruits...................29
Sweet Potato Breakfast Hash with Eggs 29
Salmon Bruschetta on Whole Grain Bread.......30
Mango Coconut Chia Pudding..............................30
Quinoa Breakfast Bowl with Berries 31
Spinach, Banana & Berry Smoothie Bowl...........31
Scrambled Tofu with Vegetables 32
Whole Grain Pancakes with Fresh Fruits............32
Banana and Almond Butter Toast......................33
Breakfast Chia Seed Pudding......................33
Greek Yogurt Parfait with Berries 34
Cottage Cheese and Pineapple Bowl...................34
Apple Cinnamon Overnight Oats 35
Egg Muffins with Vegetables 35
Tomato Basil & Guacamole Toast.......................36
Spinach and Feta Breakfast Wrap.......................36

SNACKS AND APPETIZERS

Hummus Classic......................38
Cucumber Bites with Feta and Dill 38
Cottage Cheese-Stuffed Cherry Tomatoes.......39
Roasted Red Pepper and Basil Bruschetta........39
Spinach and Cheese Stuffed Mushrooms.........40
Sweet Potato Toasts......................40
Caprese Skewers with Balsamic Glaze................41
Zucchini Chips with Parmesan.............................41
Almond & Cream Cheese Stuffed Dates..........42
Baked Carrot Fries 42

SALADS

Greek Salad with Feta and Olives 44
Quinoa and Black Bean Salad 44
Spinach and Strawberry Salad 45
Chickpea and Avocado Salad 45
Cucumber and Tomato Salad.................................46
Kale and Apple Salad 46
Mixed Green Salad..............................47
Beet and Goat Cheese Salad 47
Zucchini and Corn Salad..............................48
Carrot and Raisin Salad..............................48
Broccoli and Cranberry Salad...............................49
Watermelon and Feta Salad..................................49
Mediterranean Orzo Salad..................................50
Grilled Vegetable Salad..................................50
Chicken Avocado Salad..................................51
Cucumber and Cabbage Salad...............................51
Grilled Chicken Citrus Arugula Salad................52
Three Bean Salad with Vinaigrette 52
Caprese Salad..............................53
Sweet Potato & Black Bean Salad 53
Salmon and Quinoa Salad 54
Shrimp and Avocado Salad 54

MAIN DISHES

Lemon Herb Grilled Chicken...............................56
Baked Salmon with Dill Yogurt Sauce................56
Quinoa-Stuffed Bell Peppers..................................57
Garlic-Lemon Shrimp Skewers.............................57

DASH DIET
Cookbook for Beginners

1800 Days of Delicious Low-Sodium Recipes to Lower Blood Pressure and
Enhance Health. Includes Full-Color Photos and
a Comprehensive 30-day Meal Plan

by Christopher Donovan

Copyright © 2024 by Christopher Donovan. All rights reserved.

Title: "Dash Diet Cookbook for Beginners: 1800 Days of Delicious Low-Sodium Recipes to Lower Blood Pressure and Enhance Health. Includes Full-Color Photos and a Comprehensive 30-day Meal Plan."

This book is created to provide general information about the Dash diet and culinary recommendations for lowering blood pressure and improving health. All content, including recipes, instructions, and photographs, are the intellectual property of Christopher Donovan and are protected under copyright law. Unauthorized reproduction, duplication, or transmission of any part of this publication is strictly prohibited. This publication is intended for personal use only and is not to be used as a substitute for professional medical advice. Before starting any new diet or health regimen, especially if you have specific medical conditions or needs, consulting with a qualified healthcare provider is recommended. The author and publisher disclaim all liability for any damages or complications that may arise from the use of the information provided. This book is meant solely for informational purposes and is presented without any guarantees of accuracy or timeliness. Use of this information is at the reader's own risk. Trademarks mentioned are used only for identification and explanation without intent to infringe. No affiliation or endorsement by trademark owners is implied or should be inferred.

Tofu Stir-Fry with Vegetables 58
Lentil and Vegetable Shepherd's Pie 58
Grilled Turkey Burgers 59
Baked Cod with Tomatoes 59
Black Bean and Sweet Potato Enchiladas 60
Chicken and Vegetable Kabobs 60
Stuffed Zucchini Boats 61
Ginger-Soy Glazed Tofu 61
Herb-Crusted Tilapia 62
Whole Wheat Eggplant Parmesan 62
Spaghetti Squash with Turkey Meatballs 63
Zucchini Noodles with Grilled Chicken 63
Lemon-Honey Glazed Red Fish 64
Broiled Sea Bass with Citrus Salsa 64
Chickpea and Spinach Curry 65
Mediterranean Quinoa with Shrimp 65
Vegetable Paella with Saffron 66
Baked Lemon Garlic Tofu 66
Grilled Fish Tacos with Mango Salsa 67
Barley Risotto with Mushrooms 67
Greek Chicken Souvlaki 68
Thai Basil Tofu 68
Butternut Squash and Black Bean Chili 69
Sesame-Crusted Ahi Tuna 69
Chicken Stir-Fry with Broccoli and Carrots 70
Lemon Garlic Shrimp with Asparagus 70

SIDE DISHES

Lemon Garlic Roasted Cauliflower 72
Steamed Green Beans with Lemon 72
Mashed Cauliflower with Chives 73
Quinoa Pilaf with Vegetables 73
Honey Roasted Carrots with Garlic 74
Sweet Potato Wedges with Paprika 74
Brown Rice with Herbs 75
Balsamic Glazed Roasted Beets 75
Sautéed Spinach with Garlic 76
Broccoli with Lemon Zest 76
Cauliflower Rice with Parsley 77
Grilled Asparagus with Olive Oil 77
Wild Rice with Mushrooms 78
Whole Wheat Spaghetti & Cherry Tomatoes .. 78

DESSERTS

Baked Apples with Cinnamon and Walnuts 80
Baked Pears with Honey and Almonds 80
Strawberries and Cream 81

Dark Chocolate Avocado Mousse 81
Fresh Fruit Salad with Mint 82
Almond Butter Cookies 82
Lemon Ricotta Cheesecake 83
Banana Oatmeal Cookies 83
Strawberry Banana Sorbet 84
Blueberry Almond Crumble 84
Mango Coconut Tapioca 85
Raspberry Chia Jam 85
Apple Cinnamon Bites 86
Peach Yogurt Popsicles 86

DRINKS AND SMOOTHIES

Green Detox Smoothie 88
Berry Banana Smoothie 88
Mango Lassi 89
Iced Green Tea with Mint 89
Citrus and Berry Infused Water 90
Carrot Orange Ginger Juice 90
Pineapple Spinach Smoothie 91
Watermelon Mint Cooler 91
Beetroot and Apple Juice 92
Tropical Coconut Smoothie 92
Strawberry Lemonade 93
Classic Lemonade 93
Avocado Banana Smoothie 94
Cucumber Mint Cooler 94

SAUCES AND DRESSINGS

Balsamic Vinaigrette 96
Tomato Basil Sauce 96
Lemon Herb Yogurt Dressing 97
Lemon Tahini Dressing 97
Avocado Lime Dressing 98
Honey Mustard Dressing 98
Smoky Chipotle Yogurt Sauce 99
Cilantro Lime Dressing 99
Spicy Peanut Sauce 100
Roasted Red Pepper Sauce 100

EPILOGUE

Table of ingredient substitutions 101
Your next steps 102

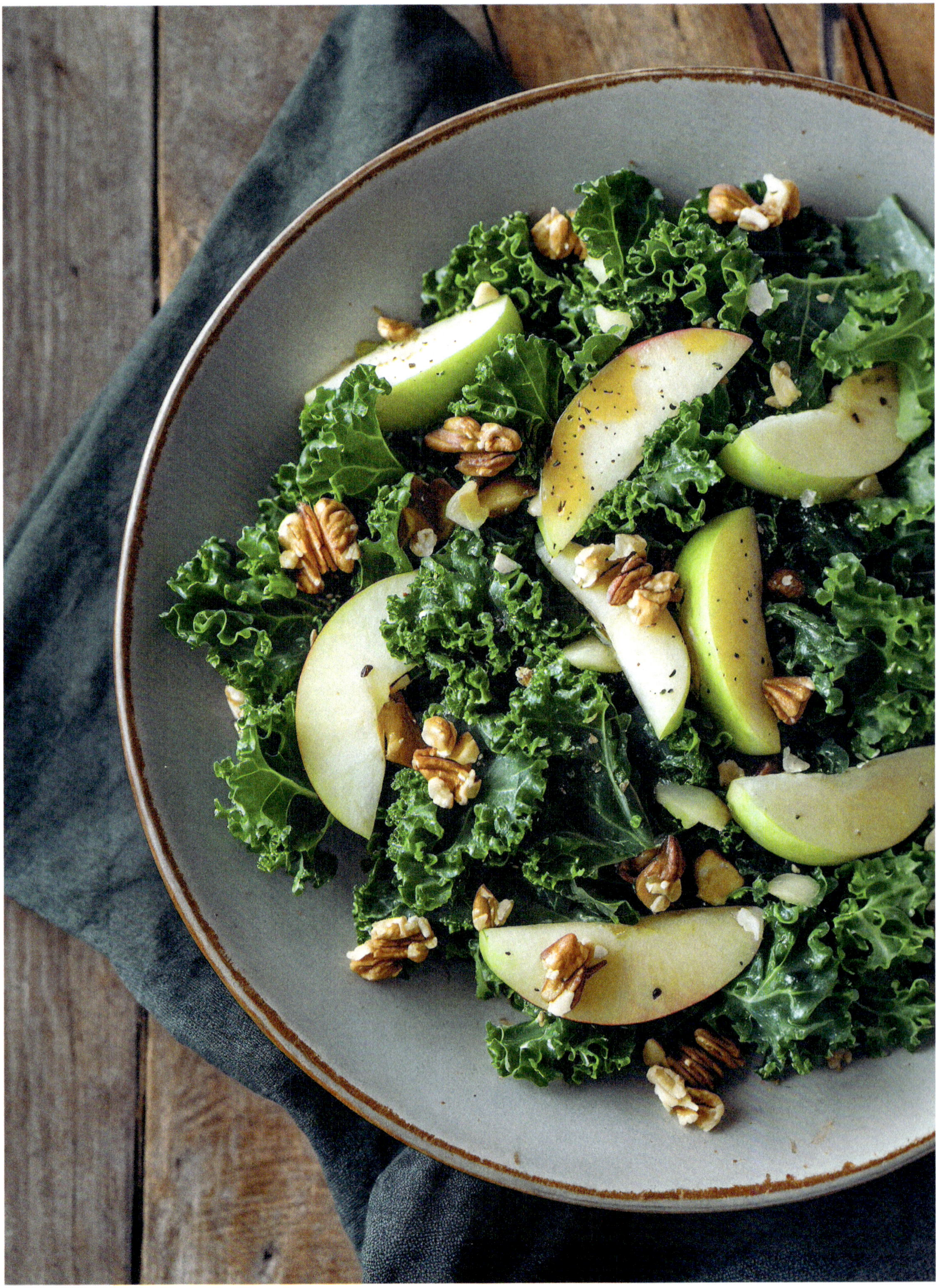

INTRODUCTION

Imagine being able to control your blood pressure, reduce the risk of heart disease, and improve your overall health—all through the food you eat. This is what the DASH Diet offers.

This book is more than just a collection of recipes—it's your guide to changing your eating habits. Here, you will find information about what the DASH Diet is, its fundamentals, who it is designed for, which foods should be included in your daily diet, and which should be limited.

Additionally, you will find a 30-day meal plan, instructions for creating your own meal plans, and numerous delicious and easy-to-prepare recipes along with nutritional values, ingredients, cooking techniques, and vivid photographs of these wonderful dishes.

WHAT IS THE DASH DIET?

The DASH Diet, an acronym for Dietary Approaches to Stop Hypertension, was developed in the early 1990s through a series of studies by the National Institutes of Health in the United States. This research aimed to identify dietary strategies to lower blood pressure without the need for medication. The findings were clear: increased consumption of fruits, vegetables, and low-fat dairy products, along with decreased intake of fatty foods, red meats, sweets, and salt, significantly lowered blood pressure. Subsequent studies also showed that the DASH Diet could reduce cholesterol levels and decrease the risk of developing cardiovascular diseases.

Today, the DASH Diet is endorsed by various government health organizations and medical societies not only for its effectiveness in managing hypertension but also for controlling cholesterol levels and aiding in the prevention of conditions such as type 2 diabetes and obesity.

THE BASICS OF THE DASH DIET AND ITS HEALTH BENEFITS

The DASH diet helps establish a heart-healthy eating pattern for life. There's no need for any special foods or drinks; dietary items are available in any grocery store and most restaurants. It's all about your choices. If you're following the DASH diet, it's important to choose foods rich in potassium, calcium, magnesium, fiber, and protein while limiting the intake of trans fats and high amounts of salt.

The DASH diet is based on eating whole, nutrient-rich foods, such as fruits, vegetables, whole grains, and low-fat dairy products, while limiting salt, sugar, and saturated fats. This way of eating ensures you get plenty of essential vitamins, minerals, fiber, and antioxidants that are important for health.

Studies have shown that the DASH Diet effectively lowers levels of LDL (bad) cholesterol and reduces the risk of cardiovascular diseases such as heart attacks and strokes. It helps regulate blood pressure because it is low in sodium and high in potassium, calcium, magnesium, and plant-based proteins. Overall, by focusing on minimally processed whole foods, the DASH Diet provides a well-balanced nutritional approach for improving overall health, preventing chronic diseases, and promoting longevity.

THE DASH DIET IS RECOMMENDED FOR:

INDIVIDUALS WITH HYPERTENSION:

The diet helps to reduce high blood pressure by promoting foods rich in potassium, calcium, and magnesium, which help to lower blood pressure by easing tension in blood vessel walls and reducing the impact of sodium.

BLOOD SUGAR CONTROL:

The DASH Diet emphasizes the consumption of complex carbohydrates and fiber-rich foods, which play a critical role in stabilizing blood sugar levels. This focus is especially beneficial for individuals with diabetes or insulin resistance as it helps prevent sudden spikes in blood glucose. By prioritizing whole grains, fruits, and vegetables over simple sugars, the diet supports a steady, healthy metabolic response.

WEIGHT MANAGEMENT:

The DASH Diet promotes healthy weight control by emphasizing whole foods over processed ones, which are often lower in calories and richer in nutrients. The high fiber content in fruits, vegetables, and whole grains ensures a feeling of fullness, helping to reduce overall calorie intake without feeling hungry. Effective weight management is crucial not only for maintaining overall health but also as a preventative measure against hypertension.

GENERAL HEALTH AND PREVENTION:

The DASH Diet is also suitable for perfectly healthy individuals who aim to maintain their health and prevent future diseases through a balanced and nutritious diet. This dietary approach is comprehensive, addressing multiple health concerns and suitable for a wide range of individuals, making it an ideal choice for anyone looking to improve their health through dietary changes.

DASH DIET & SODIUM

Sodium is a mineral that is critical in various bodily functions, including nerve signal transmission and muscle contraction. However, excessive consumption of sodium, primarily in the form of salt, can negatively impact health, especially the cardiovascular system. While salt enhances flavor and preserves food, excessive salt intake is linked to hypertension, heart disease, stroke, and other health complications.

The DASH diet emphasizes the importance of moderate sodium intake to promote optimal heart health. By reducing salt consumption and choosing low-sodium products, individuals can effectively manage their blood pressure and reduce the risk of cardiovascular diseases.

It's essential to understand that, according to some independent estimates, 75% of salt consumption typically comes from processed or ready-made foods found in supermarkets rather than from salt added during cooking. Therefore, read food labels and choose options that are low in sodium or without added salt. Avoid adding salt when cooking rice, pasta, or hot cereals. Combine different dishes that do not include salt in their recipes. Eat less restaurant food, or when dining out, request dishes with less salt and don't add salt to your order.

The standard DASH diet limits salt intake to 2300 milligrams (mg) per day, which is roughly equivalent to the amount of sodium in 1 teaspoon of table salt. However, for better blood pressure management, a target sodium level of 1500 mg per day or less is recommended. It is also advised not to completely eliminate sodium as it plays an important role in the body. Sodium helps regulate body fluids and supports the normal functioning of the nervous system and muscles, which is particularly important if you are actively engaged in sports. You can choose the diet version that best suits your health needs. If you are unsure about the appropriate level of sodium for yourself, it is advisable to consult with a dietitian or doctor to get advice tailored to your specific health needs.

For those accustomed to high-salt foods, reducing salt intake may initially make food taste bland as taste buds have adapted to high salt levels. However, over time, taste buds will adjust to lower salt levels, usually within several weeks to a month. After this adaptation period, you'll likely discover a wider range of natural flavors in foods once overshadowed by salt.

RECOMMENDED FOODS FOR THE DASH DIET

FRUITS AND VEGETABLES: These foods are rich in fiber, vitamins, and minerals that support heart health and help lower blood pressure. They also contain antioxidants that may protect you from cardiovascular diseases.

WHOLE GRAINS: These are foods made from the entire grain kernel, which is either unprocessed or minimally processed. Include whole grain bread, whole grain cereals, whole wheat pasta, and whole grain cereals in your diet. They contain more fiber, vitamins, and minerals than products made from white flour because they retain all the beneficial components of the grain, which are rich in fiber, helping to lower cholesterol levels.

LEAN PROTEIN SOURCES: Skinless poultry, fish, tofu, and legumes - these foods are important protein sources while being lower in saturated fats that can raise cholesterol levels.

LOW-FAT DAIRY: Low-fat milk, yogurt, and cheese provide calcium and protein but have less saturated fat than their full-fat counterparts.

HEALTHY FATS: Olive oil and avocados contain healthy fats that support heart health.

LEGUMES AND PULSES: Items like lentils, chickpeas, flaxseeds, and chia seeds are excellent for fiber and protein, contributing to satiety and aiding in cholesterol management.

NUTS AND SEEDS: Almonds, walnuts, flaxseeds, and pumpkin seeds are good sources of fats, fiber, and protein, which help keep heart disease at bay.

HERBS AND SPICES: Instead of salt, use a variety of herbs and spices to flavor your food, enhancing taste without adding sodium.

FOODS TO LIMIT ON THE DASH DIET

SODIUM (SALT): High sodium can raise blood pressure. Limit to no more than 2300 mg per day, about 1 teaspoon of salt. Ideally, aim for 1500 mg, roughly 1/2 teaspoon of salt per day.

SWEETS AND SUGAR-SWEETENED BEVERAGES: Sugary drinks, cookies, and candies are high in added sugars, which can raise cholesterol and heart disease risk.

TRANS FATS: These are unhealthy fats formed when vegetable oils are processed. They are often found in processed foods like fast food, margarine, fatty snacks, baked goods, etc. These increase heart disease risk.

RED MEATS AND PROCESSED MEATS: Bacon, sausage, beef, and pork are high in saturated fats that can raise cholesterol and blood pressure levels.

ALCOHOL: If you drink alcohol, do so in moderation. Excessive alcohol can raise blood pressure. For optimal health, consider cutting out alcohol completely.

REFINED GRAINS: Limit white bread, white rice, and pastries, which are high in calories and low in nutritional value.

CAFFEINE: Monitor your intake of caffeinated beverages, as excessive consumption can affect blood pressure levels.

STAY WELL HYDRATED

When following the DASH diet, staying well hydrated is crucial. Aim to drink around 8 glasses of water daily (about 2 liters), though this can vary based on age, gender, activity level, and health. Proper hydration aids in appetite control, boosts metabolism, enhances nutrient absorption, and reduces fluid retention, all beneficial for weight loss. It's recommended to consistently drink enough water throughout the day while on the DASH diet.

CONTRAINDICATIONS

The DASH diet is predominantly recognized as safe and beneficial for most people as it promotes a balanced diet using healthy foods. However, like any diet, it may have certain contraindications for some groups of people:

- People with certain kidney diseases: The DASH diet includes a relatively high level of potassium intake, which may not be recommended for people with kidney diseases or for those taking certain medications that affect potassium levels.

- People with allergies to certain foods: The diet recommends consuming a wide range of products, including dairy and nuts. Individuals with lactose intolerance or food allergies (for example, to nuts) may need to modify their diet, incorporating lactose-free alternatives to dairy products and seeds instead.

- People who require special nutrition due to other medical conditions or chronic diseases: Such individuals should consult with a doctor or dietitian before starting any new diet to ensure its safety and effectiveness for their specific health condition.

Overall, although the DASH diet is generally healthy, modifications under the guidance of a doctor or dietitian may be necessary considering certain medical conditions or dietary preferences or restrictions. This book contains general principles and recommendations for adopting the DASH diet as well as recipes that align with it. However, it is crucial to customize each plan to individual needs.

DAILY NUTRIENT LEVELS IN THE DASH DIET

The DASH Diet is not only effective for controlling high blood pressure but also serves as a guideline for consuming a balanced and nutrient-rich diet. This chapter delves into the "Daily Nutrient Levels" integral to the DASH Diet, focusing on the recommended intake of calories, macronutrients, and micronutrients, all tailored to promote cardiovascular health and overall well-being.

CALORIC INTAKE

The DASH Diet offers flexible caloric guidelines to accommodate individual needs, typically ranging from 1600 to 3100 calories per day based on age, gender, and activity level. This flexibility allows for personal adjustments to maintain or achieve a healthy weight.

MICRONUTRIENTS

- Potassium: One of the cornerstone recommendations of the DASH Diet is a high intake of potassium, around 4700 mg or more per day, to help lower blood pressure by counteracting the effects of sodium and reducing tension in blood vessels.

- Calcium: A daily intake of about 1000-1200 mg of calcium is advised to support bone health and the proper functioning of the heart and muscles.

- Magnesium: About 310-420 mg of magnesium per day is recommended to promote heart health and regulate blood sugar levels.

- Fiber: A fiber intake of approximately 30 grams per day is beneficial for digestive health and weight management.

MACRONUTRIENTS

- Proteins: Approximately 18% of daily calories should come from proteins. Emphasis is placed on plant-based and lean animal proteins such as poultry and fish to support muscle repair and growth.

- Fats: Fat intake should be limited to 27% of daily calories, with less than 6% from saturated fats, aiming to reduce the risk of heart disease.

- Carbohydrates: Carbohydrates should make up about 55% of daily caloric intake. Prioritize whole grains, vegetables, fruits, and legumes to enhance fiber intake and provide essential nutrients.

SODIUM INTAKE

Reducing sodium intake is crucial within the DASH Diet framework. Depending on specific health goals, sodium intake recommendations vary from 2300 mg to as low as 1500 mg per day. Lowering sodium consumption is key to managing blood pressure effectively.

DAILY NUTRIENT GUIDELINES FOR THE DASH DIET

It is important to note that these nutrient levels are general recommendations and individual needs may vary depending on factors such as age, gender, activity level, and overall health. Below, you will find a table of daily nutrient requirements based on gender and age.

	Age	Activity Level	Calories (kcal)	Proteins (g)	Carbohydrates (g)	Fats (g)	Sodium (mg)	Potassium (mg)	Calcium (mg)	Magnesium (mg)
Female	19-30	Low-Active	2000	46	250	70	<2300	>4700	1000	310
		Moderate	2200	50	275	77	<2300	>4700	1000	310
		High-Active	2400	54	300	84	<2300	>4700	1000	310
	31-50	Low-Active	1800	46	225	60	<2300	>4700	1000	320
		Moderate	2000	50	250	67	<2300	>4700	1000	320
		High-Active	2200	54	275	73	<2300	>4700	1000	320
	51+	Low-Active	1600	46	200	53	<2300	>4700	1200	320
		Moderate	1800	46	225	60	<2300	>4700	1200	320
		High-Active	2000	46	250	67	<2300	>4700	1200	320
Male	19-30	Low-Active	2400	56	300	84	<2300	>4700	1000	400
		Moderate	2600	62	325	91	<2300	>4700	1000	400
		High-Active	3100	71	375	105	<2300	>4700	1000	400
	31-50	Low-Active	2200	56	275	73	<2300	>4700	1000	420
		Moderate	2400	60	300	80	<2300	>4700	1000	420
		High-Active	2800	70	350	93	<2300	>4700	1000	420
	51+	Low-Active	2000	56	250	67	<2300	>4700	1200	420
		Moderate	2200	56	275	73	<2300	>4700	1200	420
		High-Active	2400	56	300	80	<2300	>4700	1200	420

The standard DASH diet limits salt intake to 2300 milligrams (mg) per day, which is roughly equivalent to the amount of sodium in 1 teaspoon of table salt. However, for better blood pressure management, a target sodium level of 1500 mg per day or less is recommended.

HOW TO CREATE YOUR DASH DIET MEAL PLAN

WHAT IS THE "HEALTHY PLATE RULE"?

The Healthy Plate rule is a simple way to visualize and create a balanced meal. It suggests dividing the plate into specific sections for different food groups in the right proportions.

THE COMPOSITION OF A HEALTHY PLATE

- Half of the plate: vegetables and fruits
- A quarter of the plate: whole grains (cereals, pasta, bread)
- A quarter of the plate: protein foods (lean meats, fish, legumes, eggs)

It is also recommended to add a serving of low-fat dairy products and a glass of water or another calorie-free drink.

The Healthy Plate rule is an ideal tool for visualizing the principles of the DASH diet. It helps adhere to the recommended proportions of the main food groups and control portion sizes.

1. VEGETABLES:

Eat more vegetables—the greater the variety, the better. Potatoes and fries are not considered healthy. Use healthy oils such as olive oil or cold-pressed flaxseed oil for cooking, in salads, and at the table. Limit the use of cream and butter, and avoid trans fats.

3. WHOLE GRAINS:

Choose a variety of whole grains, such as whole wheat bread, whole grain pasta, and brown rice. Limit the consumption of processed grains like white rice and white bread.

6. WATER:

Drink water, tea, or coffee without sugar. Avoid sugary drinks. It is best to drink pure water.

4. HEALTHY PROTEINS:

Prefer fish, skinless poultry, legumes, and nuts; limit the intake of red meat and cheese; avoid bacon, sausages, and other processed meats.

2. FRUITS:

Consume a variety of fruits, preferably of different colors. You can also make smoothies from them.

5. LOW-FAT DAIRY PRODUCTS:

Include low-fat dairy options in your diet to help maintain a balanced nutritional intake.

RULES FOR A BALANCED & SUCCESSFUL DASH DIET MEAL PLAN

Creating a personalized DASH diet meal plan can be a straightforward process if you follow these steps:

1. GET ACQUAINTED WITH THE BASICS OF THE DASH DIET:

Before you start planning your meals, it is important to understand the fundamental principles of the DASH diet. If you haven't read the previous chapters of the book yet, please do so as it is very important for planning this diet.

2. DETERMINE YOUR CALORIE NEEDS:

Calculate your daily calorie requirements based on your age, sex, height, weight, and activity level. This will serve as a foundation for your meal plan.

3. SET YOUR NUTRIENT TARGETS:

The DASH diet recommends specific daily targets for nutrients like total fat, saturated fat, cholesterol, sodium, potassium, calcium, magnesium, and fiber. Refer to the guidelines provided in the previous chapters to set your individual targets.

4. PLAN YOUR MEALS:

Divide your total calorie intake into three main meals and one or two snacks. Aim for a balanced distribution of nutrients throughout the day.

5. INCORPORATE DASH-FRIENDLY FOODS:

Focus on incorporating whole grains, fruits, vegetables, lean proteins, low-fat dairy, nuts, seeds, and legumes into your meals. Refer to the lists of recommended foods from the previous chapters.

6. LIMIT SODIUM INTAKE:

Pay close attention to sodium levels in your meals. Choose low-sodium or sodium-free options whenever possible and minimize processed and pre-packaged foods.

7. HYDRATE ADEQUATELY:

Drink plenty of water and other unsweetened beverages throughout the day to meet your hydration needs.

8. VARY YOUR MENU:

Rotate different DASH-friendly foods to ensure variety and prevent boredom. Experiment with new recipes and flavors to keep your diet interesting and sustainable.

9. PLAN AHEAD:

Meal prepping and batch cooking can save time and help you stick to your DASH diet plan. Prepare meals in advance or have ingredients ready for quick assembly.

10. MONITOR AND ADJUST:

Keep track of your food intake, monitor your blood pressure levels, and make adjustments to your meal plan as needed. Consult with a healthcare professional or a registered dietitian if you need personalized guidance.

Remember, consistency and adherence to the DASH diet principles are key to achieving the desired health benefits. Be patient and celebrate small victories along the way as you incorporate this nutritious eating pattern into your lifestyle.

BLOOD PRESSURE DIARY

When following a DASH diet plan, it's crucial to regularly monitor your blood pressure to assess the diet's effectiveness in reducing hypertension. Tracking allows for adjustments based on individual responses and helps tailor the diet to personal health needs. Below, you will find a table where you can record your blood pressure readings, which will assist in adjusting your diet if necessary. This tracking is crucial for creating a personalized DASH diet plan.

Date	Time	Blood pressure	Heart rate	Notes

If this journal has been filled, or if you need an additional Blood Pressure Diary, you can scan the QR code to download a Blood Pressure Diary formatted for A4 paper. You can then print it at home or at any nearby print center.

30 DAY MEAL PLAN

	BREAKFAST	LUNCH	DINNER	SNACK
Day 1	Oatmeal with Fresh Berries p.26	Broccoli and Cranberry Salad p.49	Baked Salmon with Dill Yogurt Sauce p.56 + Steamed Green Beans p.72	Avocado Banana Smoothie p.94
Day 2	Vegetable Omelet with Herbs p.27	Spinach and Strawberry Salad p.45	Tofu Stir-Fry with Vegetable p.58 + Carrot and Raisin Salad p.48	Sweet Potato Toasts p.40
Day 3	Greek Yogurt with Honey and Walnuts p.26	Three Bean Salad with Vinaigrette p.52	Zucchini Noodles with Pesto and Grilled Chicken p.63	Zucchini Chips with Parmesan p.41
Day 4	Smoothie Bowl with Spinach, Banana, and Berries p.31	Shrimp and Avocado Salad p.54	Herb-Crusted Tilapia p.62 + Lemon Garlic Roasted Cauliflower p.72	Berry Banana Smoothie p.88
Day 5	Salmon Bruschetta on Whole Grain Bread p.30	Citrus and Arugula Salad with Grilled Chicken p.52	Ginger-Soy Glazed Tofu p.61 + Mashed Cauliflower with Chives p.73	Baked Apples with Cinnamon and Walnuts p.80
Day 6	Breakfast Chia Seed Pudding with Almond Milk p.33	Greek Salad with Feta and Olives p.44	Baked Cod with Tomatoes p.59 + Brown Rice with Herbs p.75	Tomato Basil Breakfast Toast with Guacamole p.36
Day 7	Cottage Cheese with Fruits p.28	Kale and Apple Salad p.46	Tofu Stir-Fry with Vegetables p.58	Stuffed Dates with Almonds and Cream Cheese p.42
Day 8	Sweet Potato Breakfast Hash p.29	Watermelon and Feta Salad p.49	Pan-Seared Red Fish with p.64 + Grilled Asparagus with Olive Oil p.77	Baked Carrot Fries p.42 + Hummus Classic p.38
Day 9	Avocado and Egg Toast p.28	Beet and Goat Cheese Salad p.47	Broiled Sea Bass p.64 + Cucumber and Cabbage Salad p.51	Mango Lassi p.89
Day 10	Muesli with Yogurt and Fresh Fruits p.29	Chickpea and Avocado Salad p.45	Quinoa-Stuffed Bell Peppers p.57 + Garlic-Lemon Shrimp Skewers p.57	Cherry Tomatoes Stuffed with Cottage Cheese p.39

	BREAKFAST	LUNCH	DINNER	SNACK
Day 11	Spinach and Mushroom Egg White Omelet p.27	Quinoa and Black Bean Salad p.44	Eggplant Parmesan with Whole Wheat Breadcrumbs p.62 + Whole Wheat Spaghetti p.78	Fresh Fruit Salad with Mint p.82
Day 12	Cottage Cheese and Pineapple Bowl p.34	Zucchini and Corn Salad p.48	Grilled Turkey Burgers p.59 + Baked Carrot Fries p.42	Green Detox Smoothie p.88
Day 13	Quinoa Breakfast Bowl with Berries and Nuts p.31	Roasted Sweet Potato and Black Bean Salad p.53	Chickpea and Spinach Curry p.65 + Strawberries and Cream p.81	Roasted Red Pepper and Basil Bruschetta p.39
Day 14	Mango Coconut Chia Pudding p.30	Salmon and Quinoa Salad p.54	Lentil and Vegetable Shepherd's Pie p.58 + Mango Coconut Tapioca p.85	Pineapple Spinach Smoothie p.91
Day 15	Breakfast Chia Seed Pudding with Almond Milk p.33	Chicken Avocado Salad p.51	Spaghetti Squash and Turkey Meatballs p.63 + Caprese Salad p.53	Spinach and Cheese Stuffed Mushrooms p.40
Day 16	Banana and Almond Butter Toast p.33	Grilled Vegetable Salad p.50	Lemon Herb Grilled Chicken p.56 + Sweet Potato Wedges with Paprika p.74	Beetroot and Apple Juice p.92
Day 17	Egg Muffins with Vegetables p.35	Mediterranean Orzo Salad p.50	Stuffed Zucchini Boat p.61 + Cauliflower Rice with Parsley p.77	Lemon Ricotta Cheesecak p.83
Day 18	Whole Grain Pancakes with Fresh Fruits p.32	Mixed Green Salad p.47	Chicken Stir-Fry with Broccoli and Carrots p.70	Berry Banana Smoothie p.88
Day 19	Scrambled Tofu with Vegetables p.32	Carrot and Raisin Salad p.48	Butternut Squash and Black Bean Chili p.69 & Baked Pears with Honey and Almonds p.80	Cucumber Bites with Feta and Dill p.38
Day 20	Greek Yogurt Parfait with Granola and Berries p.34	Cucumber and Tomato Salad p.46	Chicken and Vegetable Kabobs p.60 + Grilled Asparagus with Olive Oil p.77	Tomato Basil Breakfast Toast with Guacamole p.36

	BREAKFAST	LUNCH	DINNER	SNACK
Day 21	Spinach and Feta Breakfast Wrap p.36	Broccoli and Cranberry Salad p.49	Mediterranean Quinoa with Sautéed Shrimp p.65	Blueberry Almond Crumble p.84
Day 22	Apple Cinnamon Overnight Oats p.35	Vegetable Paella with Saffron p.66	Sesame-Crusted Ahi Tuna p.69 + Quinoa Pilaf with Vegetables p.73	Strawberries and Cream p.81
Day 23	Greek Yogurt with Honey and Walnuts p.26	Grilled Fish Tacos with Mango Salsa p.67	Lemon Garlic Shrimp with Asparagus p.70	Green Detox Smoothie p.88
Day 24	Vegetable Omelet with Herbs p.27	Shrimp and Avocado Salad p.54	Wild Rice with Mushrooms p.78	Roasted Red Pepper and Basil Bruschetta p.39
Day 25	Sweet Potato Breakfast Hash p.29	Spinach and Strawberry Salad p.45	Thai Basil Tofu p.68 + Mixed Green Salad p.47	Banana and Almond Butter Toast p.33
Day 26	Cottage Cheese with Fruits p.28	Kale and Apple Salad p.46	Black Bean and Sweet Potato Enchiladas p.60	Breakfast Chia Seed Pudding with Almond Milk p.33
Day 27	Smoothie Bowl with Spinach, Banana, and Berries p.31	Chicken Avocado Salad p.51	Greek Chicken Souvlaki p.68 + Broccoli with Lemon Zest p.76	Mango Lassi p.89
Day 28	Avocado and Egg Toast p.28	Citrus and Arugula Salad with Grilled Chicken p.52	Barley Risotto with Mushrooms p.67 + Cucumber and Tomato Salad p.46	Avocado Banana Smoothie p.94
Day 29	Oatmeal with Fresh Berries and Nuts p.26	Watermelon and Feta Salad p.49	Baked Lemon Garlic Tofu p.66 + Honey Roasted Carrots with Garlic and Thyme p.74	Baked Pears with Honey and Almonds p.80
Day 30	Muesli with Yogurt p.29	Greek Salad with Feta and Olives p.44	Baked Cod with Tomatoes p.59 + Brown Rice with Herbs p.75	Dark Chocolate Avocado Mousse p.81

DASH DIET SHOPPING LIST

VEGETABLES

- ○ Broccoli
- ○ Carrots
- ○ Cauliflower
- ○ Cucumbers
- ○ Spinach
- ○ Kale
- ○ Lettuce
- ○ Bell peppers
- ○ Tomatoes
- ○ Zucchini
- ○ Brussels sprouts
- ○ Green beans
- ○ Eggplant
- ○ Onions
- ○ Mushrooms
- ○ Sweet potatoes
- ○ Red onion
- ○ Cabbage
- ○ Beets
- ○ Parsley
- ○ Dill
- ○ Cilantro
- ○ Green onions

WHOLE GRAINS

- ○ Brown rice
- ○ Quinoa
- ○ Oats
- ○ Barley
- ○ Whole wheat bread
- ○ Whole grain pasta
- ○ Whole grain flour
- ○ Orzo pasta

MEAT AND FISH

- ○ Chicken fillet
- ○ Turkey breast
- ○ Red fish
- ○ White fish
- ○ Shrimp

DAIRY AND EGGS

- ○ Low-fat milk
- ○ Low-fat Greek yogurt
- ○ Low-fat cottage cheese
- ○ Eggs
- ○ Low-fat cream cheese
- ○ Low-fat mozzarella
- ○ Low-fat feta cheese
- ○ Low-fat vegan yogurt

FRUIT

- ○ Apples
- ○ Bananas
- ○ Oranges
- ○ Strawberries
- ○ Blueberries
- ○ Raspberries
- ○ Grapefruits
- ○ Grapes
- ○ Kiwi
- ○ Mango
- ○ Watermelon
- ○ Cantaloupe
- ○ Peaches
- ○ Pears
- ○ Pineapples
- ○ Lemon
- ○ Lime

NUTS AND SEEDS

- ○ Almonds
- ○ Walnuts
- ○ Pistachios
- ○ Chia seeds
- ○ Flaxseeds
- ○ Pumpkin seeds
- ○ Sunflower seeds
- ○ Raisins

LEGUMES

- ○ Black beans
- ○ Lentils
- ○ Chickpeas
- ○ Kidney beans
- ○ Pinto beans
- ○ Green beans

FAT AND OIL

- ○ Olive oil
- ○ Avocado
- ○ Canola oil
- ○ Coconut milk
- ○ Unsweet almond milk

OTHER

- ○ Garlic
- ○ Ground cinnamon
- ○ Ground black pepper
- ○ Ground cumin
- ○ Ground turmeric
- ○ Ground coriander
- ○ Garam masala
- ○ Paprika
- ○ Dried thyme
- ○ Dijon mustard
- ○ Balsamic vinegar
- ○ Red wine vinegar
- ○ Apple cider vinegar
- ○ Honey
- ○ Maple syrup
- ○ Vanilla extract
- ○ Shredded coconut
- ○ Ginger

DASH DIET AND WEIGHT LOSS

The healthy eating plan known as the DASH diet was initially developed to treat or prevent high blood pressure. However, research has shown that it is also effective for weight loss. Researchers have found that high blood pressure is less common among those who limit their consumption of red meat, sodium, fats, and refined sugar.

For example, a study published in the "Archives of Internal Medicine" in 2010 found that adherence to the DASH diet aids in weight loss and improves health, especially when the diet is combined with a low-sodium intake. Also, a review in the "American Heart Journal" in 2017 noted that the DASH diet reduces the risk of heart disease and promotes weight loss by limiting high-calorie foods and focusing on nutrient-rich products. A 2016 study in the "Journal of the Academy of Nutrition and Dietetics" showed that followers of the DASH diet have a lower risk of developing metabolic syndrome, including excess weight and obesity.

The DASH diet can help with weight loss, but it's important to remember that creating a calorie deficit by consuming fewer calories than expended is necessary. The main idea is not just to reduce the amount of food but to consume products that provide the body with all the necessary nutrients for normal and healthy functioning while being low in calories.

The DASH diet can help you lose weight due to several factors:

1. **INCREASING SATIETY:** The DASH diet recommends consuming plenty of fiber-rich foods such as fruits, vegetables, whole grains, and lean protein sources that have low energy density but high nutritional value. The diet also advises adequate intake of lean protein sources like skinless poultry, fish, and legumes. These foods provide a lasting feeling of fullness, helping to reduce overall calorie intake. It is important to find the right balance so that the body gets enough essential nutrients with minimal calories while staying fuller for longer.

2. **CALORIE CONTROL:** The DASH diet limits the intake of fats, especially saturated and trans fats, as well as sweets and sugary drinks, which are sources of excess calories. Consuming fewer processed foods and more natural ingredients helps reduce the intake of hidden calories and unhealthy fats, while providing all the necessary elements for healthy functioning.

3. **SODIUM REDUCTION:** Limiting sodium helps reduce fluid retention in the body, aiding in weight loss. Furthermore, consuming less salty food helps reduce overall calorie intake, as salty food often stimulates the appetite.

4. **BALANCED DIET:** The diet ensures a balanced ratio of nutrients, which is important for supporting metabolism and reducing hunger.

RECOMMENDATIONS FOR SUCCESSFUL WEIGHT LOSS ON THE DASH DIET

WHAT TO DO:
Eat frequently and in small portions to maintain steady energy and avoid overeating. Include high-fiber foods such as fruits, vegetables, and whole grains to provide your body with the necessary nutrients. Include lean proteins such as skinless chicken, fish, legumes, tofu, and low-fat dairy to stay full and maintain muscle mass. Control portion sizes using smaller plates and monitor how much you eat to avoid excess calorie consumption. Stay well hydrated by drinking plenty of clean water, as it helps control appetite and maintain a fast metabolism. Plan your meals in advance to avoid unhealthy choices at the last minute.

WHAT NOT TO DO:
Do not skip meals. Skipping meals can lead to overeating later and decreased energy levels. Do not consume too much salt. Avoid adding salt to dishes; it's better to use lemon juice, herbs, and spices to enhance flavor. Do not overeat even healthy foods. Remember portion control even when eating healthy products. Do not ignore physical activity. Combine healthy eating with regular physical activity for better weight loss results.

WHAT TO WATCH FOR:
Include a variety of foods in your diet to ensure you're getting all necessary vitamins and minerals. Listen to your body's signals of hunger and fullness to avoid overeating. Regularly weigh yourself and measure your body to track progress and make necessary diet adjustments.

By following these simple tips, you can effectively manage your weight and enjoy a healthy and balanced diet. Below, you will find a table with daily nutrient standards for weight loss.

	Age	Activity Level	Calories (kcal)	Proteins (g)	Carbohydrates (g)	Fats (g)	Sodium (mg)	Potassium (mg)	Calcium (mg)	Magnesium (mg)
Female	19-30	Moderate	2000	50	250	67	<1500	>4700	1000	310
Female	19-30	High-Active	2200	54	275	73	<1500	>4700	1000	310
Female	31-50	Moderate	1900	50	238	63	<1500	>4700	1000	320
Female	31-50	High-Active	2100	54	263	70	<1500	>4700	1000	320
Female	51+	Moderate	1800	46	225	60	<1500	>4700	1200	320
Female	51+	High-Active	2000	46	250	67	<1500	>4700	1200	320
Male	19-30	Moderate	2600	62	325	87	<1500	>4700	1000	400
Male	19-30	High-Active	2800	70	350	93	<1500	>4700	1000	400
Male	31-50	Moderate	2400	60	300	80	<1500	>4700	1000	420
Male	31-50	High-Active	2600	65	325	87	<1500	>4700	1000	420
Male	51+	Moderate	2200	56	275	73	<1500	>4700	1200	420
Male	51+	High-Active	2400	56	300	80	<1500	>4700	1200	420

Remember, these nutrient levels are general recommendations, and individual needs may vary depending on individual requirements, weight, chronic conditions, and your activity level.

MEASUREMENT CONVERSION CHART

US Standard	Metric ≈
1/8 teaspoon	0.5 mL
1/4 teaspoon	1 mL
1/2 teaspoon	2 mL
3/4 teaspoon	4 mL
1 teaspoon	5 mL
1 tablespoon	15 mL
1/4 cup	59 mL
1/2 cup	118 mL
3/4 cup	177 mL
1 cup	235 mL
2 cups	475 mL
3 cups	700 mL
4 cups	1 L

UD1:G8S Standard	US oz	Metric ≈
2 tablespoons	1 fl. oz.	30 mL
1/4 cup	2 fl. oz.	60 mL
1/2 cup	4 fl. oz.	120 mL
1 cup	8 fl. oz.	240 mL
1 1/2 cups	12 fl. oz.	355 mL
2 cups or 1 pint	16 fl. oz.	475 mL
4 cups or 1 quart	32 fl. oz.	1 L
1 gallon	128 fl. oz.	4 L

Fahrenheit (°F)	Celsius (°C) ≈
225°F	107°C
250°F	120°C
275°F	135°C
300°F	150°C
325°F	160°C
350°F	180°C
375°F	190°C
400°F	205°C
425°F	220°C
450°F	235°C
475°F	245°C
500°F	260°C

US Standard	Metric ≈
1 ounce	28 g
2 ounces	57 g
5 ounces	142 g
10 ounces	284 g
15 ounces	425 g
16 ounces (1 pound)	455 g
1.5 pounds	680 g
2 pounds	907 g

DISH SYMBOLS EXPLANATION

- **VG** • Vegan dishes - These dishes contain no animal products or by-products. For example, they do not include eggs, milk, cheese, honey, etc.
- **VT** • Vegetarian dishes - These dishes may include dairy products, such as milk and cheese, as well as eggs and honey. However, they do not include any meat or fish.
- **SP** • Spicy dishes - These dishes have a significant level of spiciness.

BREAKFAST

RISE AND SHINE:
IT'S BREAKFAST TIME!

OATMEAL WITH FRESH BERRIES AND NUTS

2 servings | 15 min | 230 kcal

- Rolled oats: 80 g
- Water, 1 cup ≈ 240 ml
- Unsweetened almond milk or low-fat milk, 1/2 cup ≈ 120 ml
- Fresh berries (blueberries, strawberries, raspberries) ≈ 100 g
- Almonds, sliced or chopped: 30 g
- Honey or maple syrup (optional), 1 tablespoon ≈ 15 ml
- Ground cinnamon, 1/4 tsp ≈ 1 g
- No salt

PREPARATION 5 min:

Measure out all ingredients. Rinse berries and chop if necessary (e.g., strawberries). Slice or chop almonds.

COOKING 8 min:

In a medium saucepan, bring water to a boil. Add oats and reduce heat to low, and simmer for 5 minutes, stirring occasionally. Mix in the almond milk and continue to cook for another 3 minutes, or until the oats are soft and the mixture has thickened. Remove from heat and let sit for 1 minute. Stir in cinnamon and sweetener (if using).

ASSEMBLY 5 min:

Serve the oatmeal in bowls. Top with fresh berries and almonds. Drizzle with honey or maple syrup if desired.

CAL	230 kcal	SODIUM	80 mg
CARBS	35 g	POTASSIUM	300 mg
PROTEIN	6 g	CALCIUM	200 mg
FAT	8 g	MAGNESIUM	60 g

per serving

GREEK YOGURT WITH HONEY AND WALNUTS

1 servings | 7 min | 190 kcal

- Low-fat Greek yogurt or plant-based yogurt: 150 g
- Honey, 1 tablespoon ≈ 15 ml
- Walnuts, chopped: 30 g
- No salt

PREPARATION 5 min:

If the walnuts are not already chopped, chop them into smaller pieces. Measure out the Greek yogurt into a serving bowl.

ASSEMBLY 2 min:

Drizzle the honey over the Greek yogurt. Sprinkle the chopped walnuts on top.

CAL	190 kcal	SODIUM	50 mg
CARBS	18 g	POTASSIUM	250 mg
PROTEIN	12 g	CALCIUM	150 g
FAT	9 g	MAGNESIUM	40 g

per serving

SPINACH AND MUSHROOM EGG WHITE OMELET

2 servings | 22 min | 150 kcal

- Egg whites: 6 large
- Skim milk or unsweetened almond milk, 2 tbsp ≈ 30 ml
- Olive oil, 1 tsp ≈ 5 ml
- Fresh mushrooms, sliced: 100 g
- Fresh spinach: 60 g
- Onion, finely chopped: 50 g
- Salt: a pinch
- Ground black pepper, 1/2 tsp ≈ 2 g
- Low-fat cheese (optional): 30 g
- Pinch of salt

PREPARATION 10 min:

Wash and chop the spinach, slice the mushrooms, and finely chop the onion. In a mixing bowl, whisk together egg whites, milk, salt, and pepper until frothy.

COOKING 10 min:

Heat olive oil in a skillet over medium heat. Sauté onions and mushrooms until golden, then add spinach and cook until wilted. Pour beaten egg whites over the vegetables, letting the edges set. Tilt the pan to spread uncooked eggs. Sprinkle cheese on top, fold the omelet, reduce heat, and cook until the cheese melts and the omelet sets.

ASSEMBLY 2 min:

Slide the omelet onto a plate. Optionally garnish with additional pepper or fresh herbs before serving.

CAL	150 kcal	SODIUM	170 mg
CARBS	5 g	POTASSIUM	450 mg
PROTEIN	20 g	CALCIUM	80 g
FAT	5 g	MAGNESIUM	20 g

per serving

VEGETABLE OMELET WITH HERBS

1 servings | 25 min | 240 kcal

- Eggs, 3 large
- Red bell pepper, 1 small ≈ 120 g
- Zucchini, 1 small ≈ 120 g
- Cherry tomatoes, 100 g
- Spinach, 50 g
- Low-fat milk, 2 tablespoons ≈ 30 ml
- Olive oil, 1 teaspoon ≈ 5 ml
- Fresh parsley, 10 g
- Fresh chives, 10 g
- Black pepper, a pinch
- No salt

PREPARATION 10 min:

Wash and dice the red bell pepper and zucchini. Halve the cherry tomatoes. Chop the spinach, parsley, and chives.

COOKING 10 min:

In a bowl, beat the eggs with the low-fat milk until well mixed. Heat the olive oil in a non-stick skillet over medium heat. Add the red bell pepper and zucchini, and cook for about 3-4 minutes until they start to soften. Add the cherry tomatoes and spinach, cooking for another 2 minutes.

ASSEMBLY 5 min:

Pour the egg mixture into the skillet, ensuring it covers all the vegetables. Cook for about 3-4 minutes, or until the eggs are set. Sprinkle the chopped parsley, chives, and black pepper over the omelet. Fold the omelet in half and transfer it to a plate.

CAL	240 kcal	SODIUM	140 mg
CARBS	11 g	POTASSIUM	710 mg
PROTEIN	18 g	CALCIUM	110 g
FAT	14 g	MAGNESIUM	45 g

per serving

AVOCADO AND EGG TOAST

1 servings | 20 min | 400 kcal

- Whole grain bread, 2 slices
- Avocado, 1 medium ≈ 150 g
- Eggs, 2 large
- Lemon juice, 1 teaspoon ≈ 5 ml
- Olive oil, 1 teaspoon ≈ 5 ml
- Fresh cilantro, 10 g
- Black pepper, a pinch
- No salt

PREPARATION 10 min:

Toast the slices of whole grain bread. Cut the avocado in half, remove the pit, and scoop the flesh into a bowl. Mash the avocado with a fork and mix in the lemon juice. Chop the fresh cilantro.

COOKING 5 min:

Heat the olive oil in a non-stick skillet over medium heat. Crack the eggs into a bowl, whisk them, and pour into the skillet. Cook while stirring continuously until the eggs are scrambled and cooked through, approximately 2-3 minutes.

ASSEMBLY 5 min:

Spread the mashed avocado evenly over the toasted bread slices. Divide the scrambled eggs and place them on top of each slice. Sprinkle with black pepper and chopped cilantro.

CAL	400 kcal	SODIUM	120 mg
CARBS	32 g	POTASSIUM	800 mg
PROTEIN	14 g	CALCIUM	100 mg
FAT	27 g	MAGNESIUM	50 g

per serving

COTTAGE CHEESE WITH FRUITS AND HONEY

1 servings | 15 min | 250 kcal

- Low-sodium cottage cheese, 200 g
- Fresh berries (strawberries, blueberries, raspberries), 100 g
- Banana, sliced, 1 medium ≈ 120 g
- Apple, diced, 1/2 ≈ 60 g
- Honey, 1 tablespoon ≈ 15 ml
- Walnuts, chopped, 1 tbsp ≈ 10 g
- Cinnamon, a pinch

PREPARATION 10 min:

Gather all ingredients. Wash and prepar e the berries. Slice the banana and chop the walnuts. Slice the apple, but add it in the last step to avoid browning.

ASSEMBLY 5 min:

In a bowl, place the cottage cheese. Top with the fresh berries and sliced banana. Add the sliced apple last. Drizzle with honey and sprinkle with chopped walnuts and a pinch of cinnamon.

CAL	250 kcal	SODIUM	60 mg
CARBS	34 g	POTASSIUM	500 mg
PROTEIN	15 g	CALCIUM	150 g
FAT	7 g	MAGNESIUM	40 g

per serving

MUESLI WITH YOGURT AND FRESH FRUITS

2 servings | **15 min** | **270 kcal**

- Unsweetened muesli: 100 g
- Fat-free plain yogurt: 240 ml
- Fresh berries (strawberries, raspberries, blueberries, or a mix): 75 g
- Banana, sliced: 1 medium ≈ 120 g
- Chopped nuts (almonds, walnuts): 1 tablespoon ≈ 10 g
- Cinnamon: a pinch

PREPARATION 10 min:

Gather all ingredients and prepare the fruits by washing and slicing the banana.

ASSEMBLY 5 min:

Take a serving bowl or glass and layer half of the muesli (50 g). Then add half of the yogurt (120 ml) on top of the muesli. Next, layer half of the fresh berries and banana slices over the yogurt. Repeat the layers with the remaining muesli, yogurt, and fruits. Sprinkle with chopped nuts and add a pinch of cinnamon on top.

CAL	270 kcal	SODIUM	20 mg
CARBS	42 g	POTASSIUM	450 mg
PROTEIN	10 g	CALCIUM	150 g
FAT	7 g	MAGNESIUM	40 g

per serving

SWEET POTATO BREAKFAST HASH WITH EGGS

4 servings | **42 min** | **240 kcal**

- Sweet potatoes, 400 g
- Red bell pepper, 1 medium ≈ 150 g
- Green bell pepper, 1 med. ≈ 150 g
- Red onion, diced, 1 medium ≈ 100 g
- Fresh spinach, 2 cups ≈ 60 g
- Olive oil, 2 tbsp ≈ 30 ml
- Garlic, minced, 2 cloves ≈ 6 g
- Eggs, 4 large ≈ 200 g
- Fresh parsley, chopped, 2 tbsp ≈ 8 g
- Black pepper, a pinch
- Salt, a pinch

PREPARATION 10 min:

Gather all ingredients. Peel and dice the sweet potatoes. Dice the red and green bell peppers and red onion. Mince the garlic and chop the fresh parsley. Rinse and dry the spinach.

COOKING 30 min:

Heat olive oil in a skillet on medium. Cook sweet potatoes for 10 mins until soft. Add bell peppers, onion, garlic; cook 10-15 mins until tender. Add spinach; cook 2-3 mins until wilted. Make wells in the hash, crack an egg into each, season with salt and pepper. Cover and cook 5 mins until eggs are done.

ASSEMBLY 2 min:

Sprinkle the chopped parsley over the cooked hash and eggs. Serve immediately.

CAL	240 kcal	SODIUM	170 mg
CARBS	31 g	POTASSIUM	650 mg
PROTEIN	9 g	CALCIUM	70 g
FAT	10 g	MAGNESIUM	40 g

per serving

SALMON BRUSCHETTA ON WHOLE GRAIN BREAD

1 servings | 15 min | 350 kcal

- Whole grain bread, 2 slices
- Smoked salmon, 100 g
- Avocado, 1/2 medium ≈ 75 g
- Cucumber, 1/2 medium ≈ 75 g
- Red onion, 1/4 medium ≈ 30 g
- Low-fat Greek yogurt, 2 tbsp ≈ 30 g
- Lemon juice, 1 teaspoon ≈ 5 ml
- Fresh dill, 5 g
- Black pepper, a pinch
- No salt

PREPARATION 10 min:

Toast the slices of whole grain bread. Thinly slice the cucumber and red onion. Cut the avocado in half, remove the pit, and slice the flesh. Chop the fresh dill.

ASSEMBLY 5 min:

Spread the low-fat Greek yogurt evenly on one side of each slice of toasted bread. Layer the avocado slices on the bread, followed by the smoked salmon, cucumber slices, and red onion slices. Drizzle with lemon juice and sprinkle with chopped dill and black pepper.

CAL	350 kcal	SODIUM	220 mg
CARBS	30 g	POTASSIUM	600 mg
PROTEIN	20 g	CALCIUM	90 mg
FAT	17 g	MAGNESIUM	50 g

per serving

MANGO COCONUT CHIA PUDDING

VG

4 servings | 15 min | 220 kcal

- Chia seeds, 50 g
- Coconut milk (unsweetened), 400 ml
- Maple syrup, 2 tablespoons ≈ 30 ml
- Mango, 1 large ≈ 300 g
- Vanilla extract, 1 teaspoon ≈ 5 ml
- Fresh mint leaves, 10 g (for garnish)
- No salt

PREPARATION 15 min:

Gather all ingredients. Peel and dice the mango. In a mixing bowl, combine chia seeds, coconut milk, maple syrup, and vanilla extract. Stir well to mix. Let the chia mixture sit for about 5 minutes, then stir again to prevent clumping. Cover the bowl and refrigerate for at least 4 hours, or overnight, to allow the pudding to set.

ASSEMBLY 5 min:

Once the chia pudding is set, divide it into serving bowls. Top with diced mango. Garnish with fresh mint leaves.

CAL	220 kcal	SODIUM	20 mg
CARBS	28 g	POTASSIUM	320 mg
PROTEIN	3 g	CALCIUM	80 g
FAT	11 g	MAGNESIUM	50 g

per serving

QUINOA BREAKFAST BOWL WITH BERRIES AND NUTS

4 servings | 20 min | 270 kcal

- Quinoa, 200 g
- Water, 480 ml
- Unsweetened almond milk, 240 ml
- Fresh berries - strawberries, raspberries, blueberries, or a mix, 150 g
- Banana, 1 medium ≈ 120 g
- Chopped nuts - almonds, walnuts, etc., 2 tablespoons ≈ 20 g
- Maple syrup, 2 tablespoons ≈ 30 ml
- Cinnamon, 1/2 teaspoon ≈ 2.5 g
- Vanilla extract, 1 teaspoon ≈ 5 ml
- No salt

PREPARATION 5 min:

Gather all ingredients. Rinse the quinoa thoroughly under cold water. Slice the banana.

COOKING 15 min:

In a medium saucepan, bring water to a boil. Add quinoa, reduce heat to low, cover, and simmer for about 15 minutes or until quinoa is tender and water is absorbed. Remove from heat and let it sit, covered, for 5 minutes. Fluff the quinoa with a fork. In a small saucepan, warm the almond milk over low heat. Stir in the maple syrup, cinnamon, and vanilla extract until well combined.

ASSEMBLY 5 min:

Divide the cooked quinoa into serving bowls. Pour the warm almond milk mixture over the quinoa. Top with fresh berries, banana slices, and chopped nuts.

CAL	270 kcal	SODIUM	15 mg
CARBS	44 g	POTASSIUM	400 mg
PROTEIN	7 g	CALCIUM	90 g
FAT	8 g	MAGNESIUM	80 g

per serving

SMOOTHIE BOWL WITH SPINACH, BANANA, AND BERRIES

1 servings | 20 min | 380 kcal

- Fresh spinach, 60 g
- Banana, 1 medium ≈ 120 g
- Unsweetened almond milk, 120 ml
- Fresh mixed berries (strawberries, blueberries, raspberries), 100 g
- Kiwi, 1 medium ≈ 75 g
- Granola, 50 g
- Chia seeds, 1 tablespoon ≈ 12 g
- Unsweetened shredded coconut, 1 tablespoon ≈ 7 g (optional)
- Walnuts, chopped, 1 tablespoon ≈ 10 g (optional)

PREPARATION 10 min:

Gather all ingredients. Wash the spinach and fresh berries. Peel and slice the banana and kiwi.

COOKING 5 min:

In a blender, combine the spinach, banana, and almond milk. Blend until smooth.

ASSEMBLY 2 min:

Pour the smoothie into a bowl. Top with mixed berries, kiwi slices, granola, fresh raspberries, fresh blueberries, chia seeds, shredded coconut, and chopped walnuts. Serve immediately.

CAL	380 kcal	SODIUM	80 mg
CARBS	62 g	POTASSIUM	900 mg
PROTEIN	8 g	CALCIUM	200 g
FAT	12 g	MAGNESIUM	70 g

per serving

SCRAMBLED TOFU WITH VEGETABLES

2 servings | 17 min | 180 kcal

- Firm tofu: 200 g
- Olive oil: 1 teaspoon ≈ 5 ml
- Onion, finely chopped ≈ 50 g
- Bell pepper, diced ≈ 100 g
- Fresh spinach, chopped ≈ 60 g
- Turmeric: a pinch
- Ground black pepper: a pinch
- Salt: a pinch

PREPARATION 5 min:

Drain and press the tofu to remove excess water before crumbling. Chop the onion, bell pepper, and spinach.

COOKING 10 min:

Heat the olive oil in a non-stick skillet over medium heat. Sauté the onion and bell pepper until softened, about 5 minutes. Add the crumbled tofu, turmeric, salt, and pepper. Cook for another 3 minutes, stirring occasionally. Add the chopped spinach and cook until wilted, about 2 minutes.

ASSEMBLY 2 min:

Serve the scrambled tofu warm. Optionally garnish with fresh herbs.

CAL	180 kcal	SODIUM	120 mg
CARBS	10 g	POTASSIUM	400 mg
PROTEIN	14 g	CALCIUM	200 mg
FAT	10 g	MAGNESIUM	40 g

per serving

WHOLE GRAIN PANCAKES WITH FRESH FRUITS

2 servings | 20 min | 250 kcal

- Whole grain flour: 120 g
- Baking powder: 1 teaspoon ≈ 4 g
- Low-fat milk or unsweetened almond milk: 1 cup ≈ 240 ml
- Egg: 1 large ≈ 50 g
- Olive oil: 1 tablespoon ≈ 15 ml
- Fruits (berries, banana, apple) ≈ 100 g
- Honey or maple syrup (optional): 1 tablespoon ≈ 15 ml
- No salt

PREPARATION 5 min:

Mix flour and baking powder in a bowl. In a separate bowl, whisk milk, egg, and olive oil together. Combine the wet and dry ingredients until a thick batter forms. Wash and chop the fresh fruits.

COOKING 10 min:

Heat a non-stick skillet over medium heat. Pour batter onto the skillet to form small, thick pancakes. Cook until the edges start to look set and the bottom is golden brown, about 2-3 minutes, then flip and cook the other side until golden brown, about 2-3 minutes more.

ASSEMBLY 5 min:

Serve pancakes warm, topped with fresh fruits and drizzled with honey or maple syrup if desired.

CAL	250 kcal	SODIUM	140 mg
CARBS	39 g	POTASSIUM	230 mg
PROTEIN	9 g	CALCIUM	150 g
FAT	8 g	MAGNESIUM	40 g

per serving

BANANA AND ALMOND BUTTER TOAST

2 servings · 8 min · 300 kcal

- Whole grain bread: 2 slices ≈ 60 g
- Almond butter: 2 tbsp ≈ 30 g
- Banana, sliced: 1 medium ≈ 120 g
- Honey (optional): 1 teaspoon ≈ 5 ml
- Chia seeds: 1 teaspoon ≈ 5 g
- No salt

PREPARATION 5 min:

Slice the banana. Toast the bread.

ASSEMBLY 3 min:

Spread the almond butter evenly over the toasted bread. Top with banana slices. Drizzle with honey if desired, and sprinkle with chia seeds.

CAL	300 kcal	SODIUM	70 mg
CARBS	35 g	POTASSIUM	400 mg
PROTEIN	8 g	CALCIUM	100 g
FAT	15 g	MAGNESIUM	50 g

per serving

BREAKFAST CHIA SEED PUDDING WITH ALMOND MILK

1 servings · 10 min · 220 kcal

- Chia seeds: 4 tablespoons ≈ 40 g
- Unsweetened almond milk: 1 cup ≈ 240 ml
- Honey: 1 tablespoon ≈ 15 ml
- Fresh berries (blueberries, strawberries, raspberries) ≈ 100 g
- No salt

PREPARATION 5 min:

In a bowl or jar, mix chia seeds, almond milk, and honey. Stir well to ensure the chia seeds are evenly distributed. Cover and refrigerate for at least 4 hours or overnight until the mixture thickens to a pudding-like consistency.

ASSEMBLY 5 min:

Divide the chia pudding into serving bowls or glasses. Top each serving with fresh berries.

CAL	220 kcal	SODIUM	50 mg
CARBS	20 g	POTASSIUM	250 mg
PROTEIN	6 g	CALCIUM	150 g
FAT	12 g	MAGNESIUM	60 g

per serving

GREEK YOGURT PARFAIT WITH GRANOLA AND BERRIES

2 servings | 15 min | 295 kcal

- Fat-free Greek yogurt, 240 ml
- Granola (low sugar), 100 g
- Fresh berries - strawberries, raspberries, blueberries, or a mix, 150 g
- Honey, 1 tablespoon ≈ 15 ml
- Vanilla extract, 1 teaspoon ≈ 5 ml
- Chopped nuts - almonds, walnuts, etc., 1 tablespoon ≈ 10 g
- Cinnamon, a pinch
- No salt

PREPARATION 10 min:

Gather all ingredients. Wash and dry the fresh berries. If using large strawberries, hull and slice them.

ASSEMBLY 5 min:

In a mixing bowl, combine the Greek yogurt, honey, and vanilla extract. Mix well until smooth. In a serving glass or bowl, layer half of the granola (50 g) at the bottom. Add half of the yogurt mixture (120 ml) on top of the granola. Next, layer half of the fresh berries over the yogurt. Repeat the layers with the remaining granola, yogurt mixture, and fresh berries. Sprinkle chopped nuts and a pinch of cinnamon on top.

CAL	295 kcal	SODIUM	50 mg
CARBS	43 g	POTASSIUM	450 mg
PROTEIN	15 g	CALCIUM	200 mg
FAT	7 g	MAGNESIUM	45 g

per serving

COTTAGE CHEESE AND PINEAPPLE BOWL

2 servings | 10 min | 220 kcal

- Low-fat cottage cheese: 200 g
- Pineapple chunks, fresh or canned in juice (drained) ≈ 150 g
- Honey: 1 tablespoon ≈ 15 ml
- Chopped almonds: 1 tbsp ≈ 10 g
- No salt

PREPARATION 5 min:

If using fresh pineapple (better), peel, core, and cut into chunks. If using canned pineapple, drain the juice.

ASSEMBLY 5 min:

Place the cottage cheese in a serving bowl. Top with pineapple chunks. Drizzle with honey and sprinkle with chopped almonds.

CAL	220 kcal	SODIUM	180 mg
CARBS	27 g	POTASSIUM	250 mg
PROTEIN	15 g	CALCIUM	100 g
FAT	6 g	MAGNESIUM	30 g

per serving

APPLE CINNAMON OVERNIGHT OATS

2 servings | 25 min | 320 kcal

- Rolled oats, 100 g
- Water, 240 ml
- Apple, 1 medium ≈ 180 g
- Almond milk (unsweetened), 240 ml
- Maple syrup, 1 tbsp ≈ 15 ml
- Ground cinnamon, 1 tsp ≈ 2 g
- Chopped nuts - almonds, walnuts, etc., 1 tbsp ≈ 10 g
- Raisins, 2 tbsp ≈ 30 g
- No salt

PREPARATION 10 min:

Gather all ingredients. Wash and dice the apple.

COOKING 10 min:

In a medium saucepan, bring the water to a boil. Add the rolled oats, reduce heat to low, and simmer for about 5-7 minutes, stirring occasionally to prevent lumps, or until the oats are tender and the water is absorbed. In a separate small saucepan, heat the almond milk over low heat until warm.

ASSEMBLY 5 min:

Once the oats are cooked, stir in the warm almond milk, diced apple, maple syrup, and ground cinnamon. Mix well. Divide the porridge into serving bowls and top with chopped nuts and raisins.

CAL	320 kcal	SODIUM	10 mg
CARBS	60 g	POTASSIUM	350 mg
PROTEIN	7 g	CALCIUM	150 g
FAT	7 g	MAGNESIUM	60 g

per serving

EGG MUFFINS WITH VEGETABLES

3 servings | 35 min | 220 kcal

- Eggs: 6 large
- Skim milk or unsweetened almond milk: 4 tablespoons ≈ 60 ml
- Olive oil: 2 teaspoons ≈ 10 ml
- Bell pepper, diced ≈ 100 g
- Fresh spinach, chopped ≈ 60 g
- Cherry tomatoes, halved ≈ 100 g
- Onion, finely chopped ≈ 50 g
- Ground black pepper: 1/2 tsp ≈ 2 g
- Low-fat cheese (optional), shredded ≈ 30 g
- Salt: a pinch

PREPARATION 10 min:

Preheat the oven to 180°C (350°F). Lightly grease a muffin tin with olive oil or line with paper muffin cups. Wash and chop the vegetables as described.

In a large bowl, whisk together the eggs, milk, salt, and pepper until well combined.

COOKING 20 min:

In a non-stick skillet, heat olive oil on medium. Sauté onion and bell pepper until soft, about 5 minutes. Add spinach; cook until wilted, 1-2 minutes. Remove from heat. Divide sautéed veggies and cherry tomatoes among muffin cups. Pour egg mix over veggies. Top with cheese if using.

ASSEMBLY 5 min:

Bake in the preheated oven for 15-20 minutes, or until the egg muffins are set and lightly golden. Allow to cool slightly before removing from the muffin tin.

CAL	220 kcal	SODIUM	130 mg
CARBS	6 g	POTASSIUM	150 mg
PROTEIN	14 g	CALCIUM	30 g
FAT	12 g	MAGNESIUM	10 g

per serving

TOMATO BASIL BREAKFAST TOAST WITH GUACAMOLE

4 servings | 35 min | 342 kcal

- Whole grain bread, 4 slices ≈ 200 g
- Fresh tomatoes, 2 medium ≈ 300 g
- Fresh basil leaves, 1/4 cup ≈ 10 g
- Avocado, 2 medium ≈ 300 g
- Lime juice, 1 tablespoon ≈ 15 ml (add more to taste if needed)
- Red onion, 1/4 medium ≈ 25 g
- Olive oil, 2 tsp ≈ 10 ml
- Balsamic vinegar, 2 tsp ≈ 10 ml
- Black pepper, a pinch
- No salt

PREPARATION 15 min:

Gather all ingredients. Wash and dice the tomatoes. Chop the fresh basil leaves. Halve and pit the avocados, then scoop the flesh into a bowl. Finely chop the red onion.

COOKING 15 min:

Mash the avocado with a fork until smooth. Mix in the lime juice and finely chopped red onion. Add a pinch of black pepper to taste. Toast the whole grain bread slices to your preferred level of crispiness. In a small bowl, combine the olive oil and balsamic vinegar.

ASSEMBLY 5 min:

Spread a generous layer of guacamole on each toast. Place the diced tomatoes evenly on top. Drizzle with the olive oil and balsamic vinegar mixture. Sprinkle with chopped basil and add a pinch of black pepper if desired.

CAL	342 kcal	SODIUM	105 mg
CARBS	33 g	POTASSIUM	689 mg
PROTEIN	5 g	CALCIUM	54 mg
FAT	15 g	MAGNESIUM	63 g

per serving

SPINACH AND FETA BREAKFAST WRAP

2 servings | 25 min | 270 kcal

- Whole wheat tortillas, 2 medium
- Fresh spinach, 100 g
- Low-fat feta cheese, 60 g
- Egg, 2 large
- Olive oil, 1 teaspoon ≈ 5 ml
- Cherry tomatoes, 100 g
- Black pepper, a pinch
- No salt

PREPARATION 10 min:

Gather all ingredients. Rinse the spinach and cherry tomatoes. Cut the cherry tomatoes in halves. Crumble the feta cheese.

COOKING 10 min:

In a non-stick pan, heat the olive oil over medium heat. Crack the eggs into the pan and scramble until fully cooked. Add the spinach and cook for an additional 2-3 minutes until wilted. Stir in the crumbled feta cheese and cherry tomatoes. Season with a pinch of black pepper.

ASSEMBLY 5 min:

Warm the tortillas in a microwave or on a dry skillet for a few seconds until pliable. Divide the egg, spinach, and feta mixture between the two tortillas. Roll up the tortillas, folding in the sides to enclose the filling.

CAL	270 kcal	SODIUM	240 mg
CARBS	22 g	POTASSIUM	430 mg
PROTEIN	14 g	CALCIUM	200 g
FAT	15 g	MAGNESIUM	40 g

per serving

SNACKS & APPETIZERS

BY SOME PEOPLE, THE MEAL ITSELF IS A LONG
DELAY BETWEEN THE APPETIZER
AND THE DESSERT»

GERTRUDE BERG

HUMMUS CLASSIC

4 servings | **1,5 hours** | **180 kcal**

- Dried chickpeas: 2/3 cup ≈ 120 g
- Tahini: 4 tablespoons ≈ 60 ml
- Fresh lemon juice: 2 tablespoons ≈ 30 ml
- Garlic, minced: 1-2 cloves ≈ 5 g
- Olive oil: 2 tablespoons ≈ 30 ml
- Water: 2-4 tablespoons ≈ 30-60 ml,
- Ground cumin: 1/4 teaspoon ≈ 1 g
- Paprika and olive oil for garnish (optional)
- No salt

PREPARATION 15 min:

Rinse the dried chickpeas and place them in a large bowl. Cover with plenty of water and let soak overnight, or for at least 8 hours.

COOKING 1-1,5 hours:

Drain the soaked chickpeas and place them in a large pot. Cover with fresh water and bring to a boil. Reduce heat and simmer for about 1-1.5 hours, or until the chickpeas are very tender. Drain the cooked chickpeas, reserving some of the cooking water.

ASSEMBLY 5 min:

In a food processor or blender, combine the cooked chickpeas, tahini, lemon juice, minced garlic, olive oil, cumin, and salt (if using). Blend until smooth, adding the reserved cooking water a tablespoon at a time until the desired consistency is reached. Transfer the hummus to a serving bowl and garnish with a drizzle of olive oil and a sprinkle of paprika, if desired.

CAL	180 kcal	SODIUM	20 mg
CARBS	15 g	POTASSIUM	160 mg
PROTEIN	6 g	CALCIUM	40 mg
FAT	10 g	MAGNESIUM	30 g

per serving

CUCUMBER BITES WITH FETA AND DILL

4 servings | **15 min** | **85 kcal**

- Cucumbers: 2 medium ≈ 400 g
- Feta cheese (low-fat) ≈ 70 g
- Fresh dill: 2 tablespoons ≈ 10 g
- Olive oil: 2 teaspoons ≈ 10 ml
- Fresh lemon juice: 1 tsp ≈ 5 ml
- Ground black pepper: 1/4 tsp ≈ 1 g
- No salt

PREPARATION 10 min:

Wash the cucumbers thoroughly. Slice the cucumbers into 1/2 inch thick rounds. Crumble the feta cheese and finely chop the fresh dill.

ASSEMBLY 5 min:

Arrange the cucumber slices on a serving platter. In a small bowl, mix the crumbled feta cheese with the chopped dill, olive oil, lemon juice, and ground black pepper. Spoon a small amount of the feta mixture onto each cucumber slice. Serve immediately or chill in the refrigerator until ready to serve.

CAL	85 kcal	SODIUM	100 mg
CARBS	4 g	POTASSIUM	200 mg
PROTEIN	3 g	CALCIUM	70 g
FAT	7 g	MAGNESIUM	10 g

per serving

CHERRY TOMATOES STUFFED WITH COTTAGE CHEESE

4 servings | 20 min | 85 kcal

- Cherry tomatoes, 400 g
- Low-fat cottage cheese, 200 g
- Fresh basil leaves, 10 g
- Olive oil, 1 teaspoon ≈ 5 ml
- Black pepper, a pinch
- No salt

PREPARATION 10 min:

Gather all ingredients. Rinse the cherry tomatoes and fresh basil leaves. Cut the tops off the cherry tomatoes and scoop out the seeds with a small spoon or melon baller. Finely chop the basil leaves.

ASSEMBLY 10 min:

In a mixing bowl, combine the cottage cheese, chopped basil, olive oil, and black pepper. Mix well. Using a small spoon, stuff each cherry tomato with the cottage cheese mixture. Arrange the stuffed cherry tomatoes on a serving plate.

CAL	85 kcal	SODIUM	120 mg
CARBS	7 g	POTASSIUM	250 mg
PROTEIN	8 g	CALCIUM	60 g
FAT	3 g	MAGNESIUM	10 g

per serving

ROASTED RED PEPPER AND BASIL BRUSCHETTA

4 servings | 30 min | 220 kcal

- Whole grain baguette, 1 medium ≈ 250 g
- Roasted red peppers, 2 large ≈ 200 g
- Fresh basil leaves, 10 g
- Olive oil, 2 tablespoons ≈ 30 ml
- Garlic, 2 cloves
- Balsamic vinegar, 1 tbsp ≈ 15 ml
- Black pepper, a pinch
- No salt

PREPARATION 15 min:

Gather all ingredients. Slice the baguette into 1 cm thick slices. Rinse and finely chop the basil leaves. Mince the garlic. Cut the roasted red peppers into small strips.

COOKING 10 min:

Preheat the oven to 180°C (350°F). Arrange the baguette slices on a baking sheet and brush each slice with a small amount of olive oil. Toast in the oven for 8-10 minutes, or until golden brown.

ASSEMBLY 5 min:

In a medium bowl, combine the diced roasted red peppers, minced garlic, olive oil, and balsamic vinegar. Mix well. Spread a small amount of this mixture on each toasted baguette slice. Sprinkle with chopped basil and black pepper.

CAL	220 kcal	SODIUM	150 mg
CARBS	28 g	POTASSIUM	180 mg
PROTEIN	5 g	CALCIUM	50 g
FAT	10 g	MAGNESIUM	20 g

per serving

SPINACH AND CHEESE STUFFED MUSHROOMS

4 servings | 50 min | 150 kcal

- Large mushrooms, ≈ 300 g
- Fresh spinach, 2 cups ≈ 60 g
- Low-fat cream cheese, 1/2 cup ≈ 120 g
- Low-fat mozzarella cheese, shredded, 1/2 cup ≈ 60 g
- Garlic, minced, 2 cloves ≈ 6 g
- Olive oil, 1 tablespoon ≈ 15 ml
- Black pepper, to taste
- A pinch of salt

PREPARATION 10 min:

Gather all ingredients. Remove the stems from the mushrooms and chop the fresh spinach. Mince the garlic.

COOKING 40 min:

Preheat the oven to 180°C (350°F). In a skillet, heat the olive oil over medium heat. Add the minced garlic and cook until fragrant, about 1 minute. Add the chopped spinach and cook until wilted, about 2-3 minutes. Remove from heat and let cool slightly. In a mixing bowl, combine the cooked spinach, low-fat cream cheese, shredded low-fat mozzarella cheese, black pepper, and a pinch of salt. Mix well until combined. Stuff each mushroom cap with the spinach and cheese mixture. Place the stuffed mushrooms on a baking sheet lined with parchment paper. Bake in the preheated oven for 20 minutes, or until the mushrooms are tender and the cheese is melted and golden.

CAL	150 kcal	SODIUM	160 mg
CARBS	5 g	POTASSIUM	420 mg
PROTEIN	10 g	CALCIUM	140 mg
FAT	11 g	MAGNESIUM	20 g

per serving

SWEET POTATO TOASTS

4 servings | 30 min | 85 kcal

- Sweet potatoes, 2 medium ≈ 400 g
- Avocado, mashed, 1 medium ≈ 150 g
- Cherry tomatoes, 1 cup ≈ 150 g
- Fresh spinach, 1 cup ≈ 30 g
- Feta cheese, crumbled, 1/2 cup ≈ 60 g (optional, low-fat)
- Olive oil, 1 tablespoon ≈ 15 ml
- Lemon juice, 1 tablespoon ≈ 15 ml
- Black pepper, to taste
- No salt

PREPARATION 10 min:

Gather all ingredients. Slice the sweet potatoes lengthwise into 1/4-inch thick slices. Halve the cherry tomatoes, chop the fresh spinach, and mash the avocado. If using, crumble the feta cheese.

COOKING 15 min:

Preheat the oven to 200°C (400°F). Place the sweet potato slices on a baking sheet lined with parchment paper. Brush both sides of the sweet potato slices with olive oil. Bake in the preheated oven for 15 minutes, flipping halfway through, until tender and slightly crispy.

ASSEMBLY 5 min:

Once the sweet potato slices are done, let them cool slightly. Spread mashed avocado evenly on each slice. Top with halved cherry tomatoes, chopped spinach, and crumbled feta cheese (if using). Drizzle with lemon juice and season with black pepper.

CAL	180 kcal	SODIUM	80 mg
CARBS	26 g	POTASSIUM	550 mg
PROTEIN	4 g	CALCIUM	60 g
FAT	8 g	MAGNESIUM	30 g

per serving

CAPRESE SKEWERS WITH BALSAMIC GLAZE

4 servings | 25 min | 150 kcal

- Cherry tomatoes, 1 cup ≈ 150 g
- Fresh mozzarella balls (low-fat), 1 cup ≈ 150 g
- Fresh basil leaves, 1 cup ≈ 20 g
- Balsamic vinegar, 1/4 cup ≈ 60 ml
- Honey, 1 tablespoon ≈ 15 ml
- Olive oil, 1 tablespoon ≈ 15 ml
- Black pepper, to taste
- No salt

PREPARATION 10 min:

Gather all ingredients. Rinse the cherry tomatoes and basil leaves. Drain the fresh mozzarella balls. Thread cherry tomatoes, mozzarella balls, and basil leaves alternately onto small skewers or toothpicks.

COOKING 10 min:

In a small saucepan, combine the balsamic vinegar and honey. Bring to a boil over medium heat, then reduce the heat to low and simmer until the mixture is reduced by half and has a syrupy consistency, about 5-7 minutes. Remove from heat and let cool slightly.

ASSEMBLY 5 min:

Arrange the caprese skewers on a serving platter. Drizzle with olive oil and the prepared balsamic glaze. Season with black pepper to taste.

CAL	150 kcal	SODIUM	150 mg
CARBS	11 g	POTASSIUM	200 mg
PROTEIN	8 g	CALCIUM	180 g
FAT	8 g	MAGNESIUM	15 g

per serving

ZUCCHINI CHIPS WITH PARMESAN

4 servings | 30 min | 85 kcal

- Zucchini, 2 medium ≈ 400 g
- Grated Parmesan cheese, 50 g
- Olive oil, 1 tablespoon ≈ 15 ml
- Black pepper, a pinch
- Salt, a pinch

PREPARATION 10 min:

Gather all ingredients. Rinse the zucchini and slice them into thin rounds, about 3 mm thick.

COOKING 20 min:

Preheat the oven to 220°C (425°F). Line a baking sheet with parchment paper. In a mixing bowl, toss the zucchini slices with olive oil, salt, and black pepper. Arrange the zucchini slices in a single layer on the prepared baking sheet. Sprinkle grated Parmesan cheese evenly over the zucchini slices.
Bake in the preheated oven for 15-20 minutes, or until the zucchini chips are golden and crispy.

CAL	85 kcal	SODIUM	130 mg
CARBS	4 g	POTASSIUM	250 mg
PROTEIN	4 g	CALCIUM	60 g
FAT	6 g	MAGNESIUM	15 g

per serving

STUFFED DATES WITH ALMONDS AND CREAM CHEESE

4 servings | 20 min | 170 kcal

- Medjool dates, pitted, 12 ≈ 180 g
- Low-fat cream cheese, 1/2 cup ≈ 120 g
- Whole almonds, unsalted, 12 ≈ 20 g
- Honey, 1 tbsp ≈ 15 ml (optional)
- No salt

PREPARATION 10 min:

Gather all ingredients. Pit the dates if not already pitted.

ASSEMBLY 10 min:

Slice each date lengthwise to create an opening. Fill each date with approximately 1 teaspoon of low-fat cream cheese. Press a whole almond into the cream cheese filling of each date. If desired, drizzle a small amount of honey over the stuffed dates for added sweetness.

CAL	170 kcal	SODIUM	50 mg
CARBS	28 g	POTASSIUM	250 mg
PROTEIN	4 g	CALCIUM	60 mg
FAT	5 g	MAGNESIUM	30 g

per serving

BAKED CARROT FRIES

4 servings | 37 min | 75 kcal

- Carrots, 500 g
- Olive oil, 1 tablespoon ≈ 15 ml
- Paprika, 1 teaspoon ≈ 2 g
- Garlic powder, 1 teaspoon ≈ 3 g
- Black pepper, 1/2 teaspoon ≈ 1 g
- Dried thyme, 1/2 teaspoon ≈ 1 g
- No salt

PREPARATION 10 min:

Peel the carrots and cut them into fry-shaped sticks. Preheat the oven to 200°C (392°F).

COOKING 25 min:

In a large bowl, toss the carrot sticks with olive oil, paprika, garlic powder, black pepper, and dried thyme until evenly coated. Arrange the carrot sticks in a single layer on a baking sheet lined with parchment paper. Bake in the preheated oven for 25 minutes, turning halfway through, until the carrots are tender and slightly crispy.

ASSEMBLY 2 min:

Remove the carrot fries from the oven and let them cool slightly before serving.

CAL	75 kcal	SODIUM	10 mg
CARBS	11 g	POTASSIUM	320 mg
PROTEIN	1 g	CALCIUM	30 g
FAT	3 g	MAGNESIUM	12 g

per serving

SALADS

A SALAD IS NOT A MEAL.
IT IS A STYLE.

GREEK SALAD WITH FETA AND OLIVES

4 servings   **20 min**   **150 kcal**

- Tomatoes, 4 medium ≈ 480 g
- Cucumber, 1 large ≈ 300 g
- Red bell pepper, 1 medium ≈ 120 g
- Red onion, 1/2 medium ≈ 50 g
- Kalamata olives, pitted, 20 ≈ 80 g
- Low-fat feta cheese, 100 g
- Extra virgin olive oil, 2 tablespoons ≈ 30 ml
- Lemon juice, 1 tablespoon ≈ 15 ml
- Dried oregano, 1 teaspoon ≈ 1 g
- Fresh parsley, chopped, 10 g
- Black pepper, a pinch
- No salt

PREPARATION 15 min:

Wash the tomatoes, cucumber, and red bell pepper. Dice the tomatoes and cucumber. Slice the red bell pepper and red onion thinly. Chop the parsley.

ASSEMBLY 5 min:

In a large salad bowl, combine the diced tomatoes, cucumber, sliced red bell pepper, and red onion. Add the Kalamata olives. Crumble the low-fat feta cheese over the salad. Drizzle with extra virgin olive oil and lemon juice. Sprinkle with dried oregano, chopped parsley, and a pinch of black pepper. Toss gently to mix all ingredients.

CAL	150 kcal	SODIUM	260 mg
CARBS	9 g	POTASSIUM	350 mg
PROTEIN	5 g	CALCIUM	120 mg
FAT	11 g	MAGNESIUM	20 g

per serving

QUINOA AND BLACK BEAN SALAD

4 servings   **40 min**   **290 kcal**

- Quinoa, 150 g
- Water, 300 ml
- Black beans (canned), 240 g
- Corn kernels (fresh, canned, or frozen), 150 g
- Red bell pepper, 1 medium ≈ 150 g
- Cherry tomatoes, 150 g
- Red onion, 1/4 medium ≈ 25 g
- Fresh cilantro, 10 g
- Olive oil, 2 tablespoons ≈ 30 ml
- Lime juice, 2 tablespoons ≈ 30 ml
- Ground cumin, 1 teaspoon ≈ 2 g
- Black pepper, a pinch. No salt

PREPARATION 15 min:

Gather all ingredients. Rinse quinoa under cold water, and drain black beans and corn. Prepare fresh vegetables: dice red bell pepper, red onion, halve cherry tomatoes, and finely chop cilantro.

COOKING 15 min:

In a saucepan, bring water to a boil, add quinoa, reduce heat, cover, and simmer until tender. Let it cool to room temperature.

ASSEMBLY 10 min:

In a large bowl, mix quinoa, beans, corn, diced vegetables, and cilantro. In a small bowl, combine olive oil, lime juice, cumin, and black pepper for the dressing. Drizzle the dressing over the salad and toss gently.

CAL	290 kcal	SODIUM	10 mg
CARBS	42 g	POTASSIUM	530 mg
PROTEIN	8 g	CALCIUM	50 g
FAT	10 g	MAGNESIUM	80 g

per serving

SPINACH AND STRAWBERRY SALAD

2 servings | 15 min | 190 kcal

- Fresh spinach, 200 g
- Strawberries, 200 g
- Red onion, 1/4 medium ≈ 25 g
- Walnuts, 30 g
- Balsamic vinegar, 2 tbsp ≈ 30 ml
- Olive oil, 1 tablespoon ≈ 15 ml
- Black pepper, a pinch
- No salt

PREPARATION 10 min:

Gather all ingredients. Rinse the spinach and strawberries. Hull and slice the strawberries. Thinly slice the red onion. Chop the walnuts.

ASSEMBLY 5 min:

In a large mixing bowl, combine the spinach, sliced strawberries, and red onion. In a small bowl, whisk together the balsamic vinegar, olive oil, and black pepper. Pour the dressing over the salad and toss gently to combine. Sprinkle the chopped walnuts on top.

CAL	190 kcal	SODIUM	20 mg
CARBS	14 g	POTASSIUM	550 mg
PROTEIN	3 g	CALCIUM	70 g
FAT	14 g	MAGNESIUM	60 g

per serving

CHICKPEA AND AVOCADO SALAD

2 servings | 20 min | 300 kcal

- Chickpeas (canned, drained, and rinsed), 240 g
- Avocado, 1 large ≈ 200 g
- Cherry tomatoes, 200 g
- Cucumber, 1 medium ≈ 150 g
- Red onion, 1/4 medium ≈ 25 g
- Fresh cilantro, 10 g
- Lime juice, 2 tablespoons ≈ 30 ml
- Olive oil, 1 tablespoon ≈ 15 ml
- Black pepper, a pinch.
- No salt

PREPARATION 15 min:

Gather all ingredients. Rinse and drain the chickpeas. Rinse the cherry tomatoes, cucumber, and fresh cilantro. Dice the avocado and cucumber. Halve the cherry tomatoes. Finely chop the red onion and cilantro.

ASSEMBLY 5 min:

In a large mixing bowl, combine the chickpeas, diced avocado, cherry tomatoes, cucumber, red onion, and chopped cilantro. In a small bowl, whisk together the lime juice, olive oil, and black pepper. Pour the dressing over the salad and toss gently to combine.

CAL	300 kcal	SODIUM	10 mg
CARBS	28 g	POTASSIUM	740 mg
PROTEIN	7 g	CALCIUM	60 g
FAT	20 g	MAGNESIUM	60 g

per serving

CUCUMBER AND TOMATO SALAD

4 servings | 15 min | 100 kcal

- Cucumber, 1 large ≈ 300 g
- Cherry tomatoes, 200 g
- Red onion, 1/2 medium ≈ 50 g
- Fresh parsley, 10 g
- Olive oil, 2 tablespoons ≈ 30 ml
- Red wine vinegar, 1 tbsp ≈ 15 ml
- Black pepper, a pinch
- No salt

PREPARATION 10 min:

Gather all ingredients. Rinse the cucumber, cherry tomatoes, and fresh parsley. Slice the cucumber into thin rounds. Halve the cherry tomatoes. Thinly slice the red onion. Chop the parsley.

ASSEMBLY 5 min:

In a large mixing bowl, combine the cucumber, cherry tomatoes, and red onion. Add the chopped parsley. In a small bowl, whisk together the olive oil, red wine vinegar, and black pepper. Pour the dressing over the salad and toss gently to combine.

CAL	100 kcal	SODIUM	5 mg
CARBS	8 g	POTASSIUM	200 mg
PROTEIN	1 g	CALCIUM	20 mg
FAT	7 g	MAGNESIUM	15 g

per serving

KALE AND APPLE SALAD

4 servings | 20 min | 130 kcal

- Kale, chopped, 150 g
- Apple, 1 medium ≈ 150 g
- Walnuts, chopped, 30 g
- Fresh lemon juice, 2 tbsp ≈ 30 ml
- Extra-virgin olive oil, 2 tbsp ≈ 30 ml
- Dijon mustard, 1 teaspoon ≈ 5 ml
- Honey, 1 teaspoon ≈ 5 ml
- Black pepper, to taste
- No salt

PREPARATION 10 min:

Wash and chop the kale. Core and thinly slice the apple.

COOKING 5 min:

In a small bowl, whisk together the lemon juice, extra-virgin olive oil, Dijon mustard, honey, and black pepper to make the dressing.

ASSEMBLY 5 min:

In a large salad bowl, combine the chopped kale, sliced apple, and chopped walnuts. Drizzle with the lemon dressing. Toss gently to combine.

CAL	130 kcal	SODIUM	20 mg
CARBS	9 g	POTASSIUM	200 mg
PROTEIN	2 g	CALCIUM	50 g
FAT	10 g	MAGNESIUM	20 g

per serving

MIXED GREEN SALAD

4 servings | 15 min | 170 kcal

- Mixed greens (e.g., spinach, arugula, lettuce), 200 g
- Cherry tomatoes, 200 g
- Cucumber, 1 medium ≈ 150 g
- Avocado, 1 medium ≈ 200 g
- Red onion, 1/4 medium ≈ 25 g
- Olive oil, 2 tablespoons ≈ 30 ml
- Balsamic vinegar, 1 tbsp ≈ 15 ml
- Dijon mustard, 1 teaspoon ≈ 5 ml
- Black pepper, a pinch
- No salt

PREPARATION 10 min:

Gather all ingredients. Rinse the mixed greens, cherry tomatoes, and cucumber. Slice the cucumber into thin rounds. Halve the cherry tomatoes. Peel and dice the avocado. Thinly slice the red onion.

ASSEMBLY 5 min:

In a large mixing bowl, combine the mixed greens, cherry tomatoes, cucumber, diced avocado, and red onion. In a small bowl, whisk together the olive oil, balsamic vinegar, Dijon mustard, and black pepper. Pour the dressing evenly over the salad and toss gently to combine.

CAL	170 kcal	SODIUM	15 mg
CARBS	10 g	POTASSIUM	500 mg
PROTEIN	3 g	CALCIUM	35 g
FAT	14 g	MAGNESIUM	30 g

per serving

BEET AND GOAT CHEESE SALAD

2 servings | 80 min | 200 kcal

- Beets, 3 medium ≈ 300 g
- Mixed greens (e.g., arugula, spinach, lettuce), 200 g
- Goat cheese, 100 g
- Walnuts, 30 g
- Olive oil, 2 tbsp ≈ 30 ml
- Balsamic vinegar, 1 tbsp ≈ 15 ml
- Black pepper, a pinch
- No salt

PREPARATION 25 min:

Gather all ingredients. Rinse and scrub the beets. Rinse the mixed greens.

COOKING 45 min:

Place the beets in a pot of water and bring to a boil. Reduce heat and simmer for about 45 minutes, or until the beets are tender when pierced with a fork. Let the beets cool, then peel and cut them into small wedges.

ASSEMBLY 10 min:

In a large mixing bowl, combine the mixed greens and beet wedges. Crumble the goat cheese over the salad. Chop the walnuts and sprinkle them on top. In a small bowl, whisk together the olive oil, balsamic vinegar, and black pepper. Pour the dressing over the salad and toss gently to combine.

CAL	200 kcal	SODIUM	55 mg
CARBS	14 g	POTASSIUM	400 mg
PROTEIN	5 g	CALCIUM	70 g
FAT	15 g	MAGNESIUM	25 g

per serving

ZUCCHINI AND CORN SALAD

4 servings | 20 min | 110 kcal

- Zucchini, 2 medium ≈ 400 g
- Corn kernels (canned), 200 g
- Cherry tomatoes, 200 g
- Red onion, 1/4 medium ≈ 25 g
- Fresh cilantro, 10 g
- Lime juice, 2 tablespoons ≈ 30 ml
- Olive oil, 1 tablespoon ≈ 15 ml
- Black pepper, a pinch
- No salt

PREPARATION 15 min:

Gather all ingredients. Rinse the zucchini, cherry tomatoes, and fresh cilantro. Dice the zucchini and halve the cherry tomatoes. Thinly slice the red onion. Chop the cilantro. Drain the water from the canned corn.

ASSEMBLY 5 min:

In a large mixing bowl, combine the diced zucchini, corn kernels, cherry tomatoes, and red onion. Add the chopped cilantro. In a small bowl, whisk together the lime juice, olive oil, and black pepper. Pour the dressing over the salad and toss gently to combine.

CAL	110 kcal	SODIUM	10 mg
CARBS	13 g	POTASSIUM	350 mg
PROTEIN	3 g	CALCIUM	20 mg
FAT	6 g	MAGNESIUM	25 g

per serving

CARROT AND RAISIN SALAD

4 servings | 20 min | 120 kcal

- Carrots, 4 medium ≈ 400 g
- Raisins, 1/2 cup ≈ 75 g
- Fat-free yogurt, 1/2 cup ≈ 120 ml
- Honey, 1 tablespoon ≈ 15 ml
- Lemon juice, 1 tablespoon ≈ 15 ml
- Fresh parsley, chopped, 2 tablespoons ≈ 8 g
- Black pepper, to taste
- No salt

PREPARATION 15 min:

Wash and peel the carrots. Grate the carrots. Chop the fresh parsley.

ASSEMBLY 5 min:

In a large bowl, combine the grated carrots and raisins. In a separate small bowl, mix the fat-free plain yogurt, honey, and lemon juice until well combined. Pour the dressing over the carrot and raisin mixture. Add the chopped parsley and black pepper to taste. Toss everything gently to combine.

CAL	120 kcal	SODIUM	30 mg
CARBS	26 g	POTASSIUM	360 mg
PROTEIN	3 g	CALCIUM	80 g
FAT	1 g	MAGNESIUM	20 g

per serving

BROCCOLI AND CRANBERRY SALAD

4 servings | 25 min | 135 kcal

- Broccoli florets, 300 g
- Dried cranberries, 50 g
- Red onion, 1/2 medium ≈ 50 g
- Sunflower seeds, 30 g
- Low-fat Greek yogurt, 120 ml
- Apple cider vinegar, 1 tbsp ≈ 15 ml
- Honey, 1 tbsp ≈ 20 g
- Lemon juice, 1 tbsp ≈ 15 ml
- Black pepper, a pinch
- No salt

PREPARATION 15 min:

Wash and cut the broccoli into small florets. Finely chop the red onion.

ASSEMBLY 10 min:

In a large mixing bowl, combine the broccoli florets, dried cranberries, chopped red onion, and sunflower seeds. In a separate small bowl, whisk together the low-fat Greek yogurt, apple cider vinegar, honey, lemon juice, and a pinch of black pepper until well combined. Pour the dressing over the broccoli mixture and toss until evenly coated. Let the salad sit for about 10 minutes to allow the flavors to meld before serving.

CAL	135 kcal	SODIUM	35 mg
CARBS	22 g	POTASSIUM	390 mg
PROTEIN	5 g	CALCIUM	60 g
FAT	4 g	MAGNESIUM	25 g

per serving

WATERMELON AND FETA SALAD

4 servings | 20 min | 140 kcal

- Watermelon, cubed, 500 g
- Low-sodium feta cheese, crumbled, 75 g
- Fresh mint leaves, chopped, 10 g
- Red onion, 1/4 medium ≈ 25 g
- Balsamic vinegar, 1 tbsp ≈ 15 ml
- Olive oil, 1 tbsp ≈ 15 ml
- Black pepper, a pinch
- No salt

PREPARATION 15 min:

Cube the watermelon and finely chop the red onion and fresh mint leaves. Crumble the low-sodium feta cheese.

ASSEMBLY 5 min:

In a large bowl, combine the cubed watermelon, crumbled low-sodium feta cheese, chopped mint leaves, and finely chopped red onion. Drizzle the balsamic vinegar and olive oil over the salad. Gently toss to combine, ensuring all ingredients are evenly coated. Sprinkle a pinch of black pepper on top before serving.

CAL	140 kcal	SODIUM	130 mg
CARBS	18 g	POTASSIUM	320 mg
PROTEIN	4 g	CALCIUM	110 g
FAT	6 g	MAGNESIUM	25 g

per serving

MEDITERRANEAN ORZO SALAD

4 servings | 35 min | 240 kcal

- Orzo pasta (recommended whole wheat), 200 g
- Cherry tomatoes, halved, 200 g
- Cucumber, diced, 1 medium ≈ 150 g
- Red bell pepper, 1 medium ≈ 120 g
- Red onion, 1/2 medium ≈ 50 g
- Kalamata olives, pitted, 50 g
- Low-fat feta cheese, 100 g
- Fresh parsley, 10 g
- Olive oil, 2 tablespoons ≈ 30 ml
- Lemon juice, 2 tablespoons ≈ 30 ml
- Dried oregano, 1 teaspoon ≈ 1 g
- Black pepper, a pinch
- No salt

PREPARATION 15 min:

Halve the cherry tomatoes, dice the cucumber and red bell pepper, finely chop the red onion and fresh parsley. Crumble the low-fat feta cheese and slice the Kalamata olives.

COOKING 10 min:

Cook the orzo pasta (recommended whole wheat) according to package instructions until al dente. Drain and rinse under cold water to cool.

ASSEMBLY 10 min:

Whisk together olive oil, lemon juice, dried oregano, and a pinch of black pepper in a small bowl. In a large bowl, combine cooked orzo, cherry tomatoes, cucumber, red bell pepper, red onion, Kalamata olives, and parsley. Add the dressing and toss. Sprinkle with crumbled feta and mix gently. Let the salad sit for 10 minutes to meld flavors before serving.

CAL	240 kcal	SODIUM	210 mg
CARBS	28 g	POTASSIUM	370 mg
PROTEIN	8 g	CALCIUM	120 mg
FAT	10 g	MAGNESIUM	35 g

per serving

GRILLED VEGETABLE SALAD

4 servings | 35 min | 130 kcal

- Zucchini, sliced, 1 medium ≈ 200 g
- Red bell pepper, 1 medium ≈ 120 g
- Yellow bell pepper, 1 medium
- Red onion, 1 medium ≈ 100 g
- Cherry tomatoes, 200 g
- Eggplant, sliced, 1 medium ≈ 250 g
- Olive oil, 2 tbsp ≈ 30 ml
- Balsamic vinegar, 1 tbsp ≈ 15 ml
- Fresh basil leaves, chopped, 10 g
- Garlic, minced, 2 cloves ≈ 6 g
- Black pepper, a pinch
- No salt

PREPARATION 15 min:

Slice zucchini, red and yellow bell peppers, red onion, and eggplant. Mince the garlic. Halve the cherry tomatoes.

COOKING 15 min:

Preheat the grill to medium-high heat. In a large bowl, toss the sliced vegetables with olive oil and black pepper. Grill for 5-7 minutes on each side until tender. Remove from the grill and let cool slightly.

ASSEMBLY 5 min:

In a large mixing bowl, combine grilled vegetables and cherry tomatoes. In a small bowl, mix olive oil, balsamic vinegar, minced garlic, and chopped basil to make the dressing. Dress the vegetables and toss gently. Allow the salad to sit for 5 minutes to blend flavors before serving.

CAL	130 kcal	SODIUM	15 mg
CARBS	14 g	POTASSIUM	470 mg
PROTEIN	3 g	CALCIUM	30 g
FAT	8 g	MAGNESIUM	25 g

per serving

CHICKEN AVOCADO SALAD

4 servings | 30 min | 220 kcal

- Skinless, boneless chicken breast, 200 g
- Mixed greens (e.g., spinach, arugula, lettuce), 200 g
- Avocado, diced, 1 medium ≈ 150 g
- Cherry tomatoes, halved, 150 g
- Cucumber, 1 medium ≈ 150 g
- Red onion, 1/2 medium ≈ 50 g
- Fresh cilantro, chopped, 10 g
- Olive oil, 1 tablespoon ≈ 15 ml
- Lime juice, 1 tablespoon ≈ 15 ml
- Black pepper, a pinch
- No salt

PREPARATION 10 min:

Slice the avocado, halve the cherry tomatoes, slice the cucumber and red onion, and chop the fresh cilantro.

COOKING 15 min:

Heat the olive oil in a skillet over medium heat. Season the chicken breast with a pinch of black pepper and cook for 6-7 minutes on each side until fully cooked and no longer pink inside. Remove from heat and let cool slightly, then slice the chicken into thin strips.

ASSEMBLY 5 min:

In a large mixing bowl, combine the mixed greens, cherry tomatoes, cucumber, and red onion. In a small bowl, whisk 1 tablespoon of lime juice with black pepper. Pour over the salad and toss. Top with avocado and chicken. Drizzle with the remaining lime juice.

CAL	280 kcal	SODIUM	45 mg
CARBS	12 g	POTASSIUM	960 mg
PROTEIN	22 g	CALCIUM	80 g
FAT	17 g	MAGNESIUM	40 g

per serving

CUCUMBER AND CABBAGE SALAD

4 servings | 15 min | 70 kcal

- Cabbage, 300 g
- Cucumber, 200 g
- Fresh dill, 10 g
- Lemon juice, 2 tablespoons ≈ 30 ml
- Olive oil, 1 tablespoon ≈ 15 ml
- Black pepper, a pinch
- No salt

PREPARATION 10 min:

Wash the cabbage, cucumber, and dill thoroughly. Shred the cabbage into thin strips. Slice the cucumber into thin half-moons. Finely chop the fresh dill.

ASSEMBLY 5 min:

In a large bowl, combine the shredded cabbage, sliced cucumber, and chopped dill. Drizzle the lemon juice and olive oil over the vegetables. Toss the salad well to ensure all the ingredients are evenly coated. Add a pinch of black pepper and mix again.

VG

CAL	70 kcal	SODIUM	5 mg
CARBS	7 g	POTASSIUM	250 mg
PROTEIN	1,5 g	CALCIUM	40 mg
FAT	4,5 g	MAGNESIUM	15 g

per serving

CITRUS AND ARUGULA SALAD WITH GRILLED CHICKEN

2 servings | 35 min | 470 kcal

- Skinless, boneless chicken breast, 200 g
- Arugula, 200 g
- Orange, 1 large ≈ 180 g
- Grapefruit, 1 large ≈ 230 g
- Red onion, 1/2 medium ≈ 50 g
- Avocado, 1 medium ≈ 150 g
- Olive oil, 1 tablespoon ≈ 15 ml
- Lemon juice, 1 tablespoon ≈ 15 ml
- Fresh mint leaves, 10 g
- Black pepper, a pinch
- No salt

PREPARATION 15 min:

Peel and segment the orange and grapefruit. Thinly slice the red onion. Slice the avocado. Chop the fresh mint leaves. Wash and pat dry the arugula.

COOKING 15 min:

Season the chicken breast with black pepper. Heat a grill pan over medium heat and grill the chicken for 6-7 minutes on each side or until fully cooked. Remove from the pan and let it rest for a few minutes before slicing thinly.

ASSEMBLY 5 min:

In a large salad bowl, combine the arugula, orange segments, grapefruit segments, sliced red onion, sliced avocado, and chopped mint leaves. Drizzle with olive oil and lemon juice. Toss gently to combine. Top with the sliced grilled chicken and mix gently to integrate the chicken into the salad.

CAL	470 kcal	SODIUM	75 mg
CARBS	28 g	POTASSIUM	995 mg
PROTEIN	34 g	CALCIUM	120 g
FAT	24 g	MAGNESIUM	60 g

per serving

THREE BEAN SALAD WITH VINAIGRETTE

4 servings | 25 min | 220 kcal

- Green beans, 200 g
- Kidney beans (canned), 200 g
- Chickpeas (canned), 200 g
- Red onion, 1/2 medium ≈ 50 g
- Fresh parsley, 10 g
- Olive oil, 2 tbsp ≈ 30 ml
- Apple cider vinegar, 2 tbsp ≈ 30 ml
- Dijon mustard, 1 teaspoon ≈ 5 g
- Honey, 1 teaspoon ≈ 5 g
- Black pepper, a pinch
- No salt

PREPARATION 15 min:

Trim and cut the green beans into 1-inch pieces. Thinly slice the red onion. Chop the fresh parsley. Drain and rinse the kidney beans and chickpeas.

COOKING 5 min:

Blanch the green beans in boiling water for 3 minutes, then drain and rinse under cold water to stop the cooking process.

ASSEMBLY 5 min:

In a large salad bowl, combine the green beans, kidney beans, chickpeas, sliced red onion, and chopped parsley. In a small bowl, whisk together the olive oil, apple cider vinegar, Dijon mustard, honey, and a pinch of black pepper to make the vinaigrette. Pour the vinaigrette over the bean mixture and toss gently to combine.

CAL	220 kcal	SODIUM	10 mg
CARBS	27 g	POTASSIUM	500 mg
PROTEIN	7 g	CALCIUM	60 g
FAT	8 g	MAGNESIUM	50 g

per serving

CAPRESE SALAD

4 servings | 30 min | 160 kcal

- Fresh mozzarella cheese, low-fat, 200 g
- Tomatoes, 2 large ≈ 400 g
- Fresh basil leaves, 20 g
- Balsamic vinegar, 4 tbsp ≈ 60 ml
- Honey, 1 tsp ≈ 5 g
- Olive oil, 1 tbsp ≈ 15 ml
- Black pepper, a pinch
- No salt

PREPARATION 10 min:

Slice the fresh mozzarella cheese and tomatoes into 1/4-inch thick slices. Wash and dry the basil leaves.

COOKING 15 min:

In a small saucepan, combine the balsamic vinegar and honey. Bring to a boil over medium heat, then reduce the heat to low and simmer until the mixture is reduced by half and has a syrupy consistency, about 5-7 minutes. Remove from heat and let it cool slightly.

ASSEMBLY 5 min:

On a serving platter, alternate slices of mozzarella and tomato, overlapping them slightly. Tuck basil leaves between the slices. Drizzle with olive oil and the balsamic glaze. Sprinkle with a pinch of black pepper.

CAL	160 kcal	SODIUM	75 mg
CARBS	10 g	POTASSIUM	300 mg
PROTEIN	10 g	CALCIUM	250 g
FAT	9 g	MAGNESIUM	20 g

per serving

ROASTED SWEET POTATO AND BLACK BEAN SALAD

4 servings | 50 min | 240 kcal

- Sweet potatoes, 2 medium ≈ 400 g
- Black beans (canned), drained and rinsed, 200 g
- Red onion, 1/2 medium ≈ 50 g
- Fresh cilantro, 10 g
- Pumpkin seeds, 30 g
- Olive oil, 2 tablespoons ≈ 30 ml
- Lime juice, 2 tablespoons ≈ 30 ml
- Cumin powder, 1 teaspoon ≈ 3 g
- Black pepper, a pinch
- No salt

PREPARATION 15 min:

Peel and dice the sweet potatoes into 1-inch cubes. Thinly slice the red onion. Chop the fresh cilantro.

COOKING 30 min:

Preheat the oven to 200°C (400°F). Place diced sweet potatoes on a baking sheet, drizzle with olive oil, and sprinkle with cumin and black pepper. Toss to coat. Roast for 25-30 minutes until tender and caramelized. Remove and let cool.

ASSEMBLY 5 min:

In a large salad bowl, combine the roasted sweet potatoes, black beans, sliced red onion, chopped cilantro, and pumpkin seeds. Drizzle with the remaining 1 tablespoon of olive oil and lime juice. Toss gently to combine.

CAL	240 kcal	SODIUM	10 mg
CARBS	36 g	POTASSIUM	550 mg
PROTEIN	7 g	CALCIUM	50 g
FAT	9 g	MAGNESIUM	45 g

per serving

SALMON AND QUINOA SALAD

2 servings | **45 min** | **500 kcal**

- Salmon fillet, 200 g
- Quinoa, 100 g
- Baby spinach, 100 g
- Cherry tomatoes, 200 g
- Cucumber, 1 medium ≈ 200 g
- Red onion, 1/2 medium ≈ 50 g
- Fresh parsley, 10 g
- Olive oil, 2 tablespoons ≈ 30 ml
- Lemon juice, 2 tablespoons ≈ 30 ml
- Dijon mustard, 1 teaspoon ≈ 5 g
- Black pepper, a pinch
- No salt

PREPARATION 15 min:

Rinse the quinoa under cold water. Halve the cherry tomatoes. Peel and slice the cucumber. Thinly slice the red onion. Chop the fresh parsley

COOKING 25 min:

Preheat oven to 200°C (400°F). For quinoa: Boil 200 ml of water, add quinoa, cover, and simmer on low for 15 minutes until water is absorbed. Let sit covered for 5 minutes, then fluff. Cook salmon: Place on a baking sheet, drizzle with olive oil and black pepper, and bake for 15-20 minutes at 200°C. Let cool and flake. For dressing: Whisk olive oil, lemon juice, Dijon mustard, and black pepper in a bowl.

ASSEMBLY 5 min:

In a large salad bowl, combine the cooked quinoa, baby spinach, halved cherry tomatoes, sliced cucumber, sliced red onion, and chopped parsley. Drizzle the dressing over the salad and toss gently to combine. Add the flaked salmon on top.

CAL	500 kcal	SODIUM	120 mg
CARBS	30 g	POTASSIUM	950 mg
PROTEIN	25 g	CALCIUM	100 mg
FAT	20 g	MAGNESIUM	90 g

per serving

SHRIMP AND AVOCADO SALAD

2 servings | **15 min** | **310 kcal**

- Cooked shrimp, 200 g
- Avocado, 1 medium ≈ 150 g
- Cherry tomatoes, 100 g
- Cucumber, 1 medium ≈ 200 g
- Red onion, 1/4 medium ≈ 30 g
- Olive oil, 2 tablespoons ≈ 30 ml
- Lime juice, 1 tablespoon ≈ 15 ml
- Fresh cilantro, 10 g
- Black pepper, a pinch
- No salt

PREPARATION 10 min:

Peel and devein the shrimp if not already done. Cut the avocado in half, remove the pit, and dice the flesh. Halve the cherry tomatoes. Peel and dice the cucumber. Thinly slice the red onion. Chop the fresh cilantro.

ASSEMBLY 5 min:

In a large salad bowl, combine the cooked shrimp, diced avocado, halved cherry tomatoes, diced cucumber, and sliced red onion. Drizzle with olive oil and lime juice. Add chopped cilantro and a pinch of black pepper. Toss gently to combine all ingredients evenly.

CAL	310 kcal	SODIUM	115 mg
CARBS	15 g	POTASSIUM	720 mg
PROTEIN	20 g	CALCIUM	80 g
FAT	22 g	MAGNESIUM	50 g

per serving

MAIN DISHES

THE GREATEST WEALTH IS HEALTH

VIRGIL

LEMON HERB GRILLED CHICKEN

4 servings | **35 min** | **220 kcal**

- Chicken breasts: 4 pieces, ≈ 600 g
- Olive oil: 2 tbsp, ≈ 30 ml
- Lemon juice: 2 tbsp, ≈ 30 ml
- Lemon zest: 1 tsp, ≈ 2 g
- Garlic: 3 cloves
- Fresh rosemary: 1 tbsp, ≈ 5 g
- Fresh thyme: 1 tbsp, ≈ 5 g
- Fresh parsley: 2 tbsp, ≈ 10 g
- Black pepper: 1/2 tsp, ≈ 1 g
- No salt

PREPARATION 15 min:

Peel and mince the garlic. In a bowl, combine olive oil, lemon juice, lemon zest, minced garlic, chopped rosemary, thyme, parsley, and black pepper. Mix well. Place the chicken breasts in a resealable plastic bag or shallow dish and pour the marinade over them. Ensure the chicken is well-coated. Marinate in the refrigerator for at least 30 minutes, or up to 2 hours.

COOKING 15 min:

Preheat the grill to medium-high heat. Remove the chicken from the marinade and let any excess drip off. Grill the chicken breasts for about 6-7 minutes per side, or until fully cooked and the juices run clear.

ASSEMBLY 5 min:

Remove the chicken from the grill and let it rest for a few minutes before serving. Garnish with additional fresh herbs if desired. Serve hot.

CAL	220 kcal	SODIUM	70 mg
CARBS	2 g	POTASSIUM	450 mg
PROTEIN	30 g	CALCIUM	30 mg
FAT	10 g	MAGNESIUM	25 g

per serving

BAKED SALMON WITH DILL YOGURT SAUCE

4 servings | **35 min** | **220 kcal**

- Salmon fillets: 4 pieces, ≈ 600 g
- Olive oil: 1 tbsp, ≈ 15 ml
- Lemon juice: 1 tbsp, ≈ 15 ml
- Black pepper: 1/2 tsp, ≈ 1 g
- Low-fat plain yogurt: 240 ml
- Fresh dill: 2 tbsp, ≈ 10 g
- Lemon juice: 1 tbsp, ≈ 15 ml
- Garlic: 1 clove
- Black pepper: a pinch
- No salt

PREPARATION 10 min:

Peel and mince the garlic. In a small bowl, mix the yogurt, chopped dill, lemon juice, minced garlic, and a pinch of black pepper to make the dill yogurt sauce. Set aside.

COOKING 20 min:

Preheat the oven to 200°C (400°F). Place the salmon fillets on a baking sheet lined with parchment paper. Drizzle with olive oil and lemon juice, and sprinkle with black pepper. Bake for 15-20 minutes, or until the salmon is cooked through and flakes easily with a fork.

ASSEMBLY 5 min:

Remove the salmon from the oven and let it rest for a couple of minutes. Serve each fillet with a generous spoonful of dill yogurt sauce on top. Garnish with additional fresh dill if desired. Serve hot.

CAL	300 kcal	SODIUM	70 mg
CARBS	4 g	POTASSIUM	700 mg
PROTEIN	30 g	CALCIUM	90 g
FAT	20 g	MAGNESIUM	40 g

per serving

QUINOA-STUFFED BELL PEPPERS

4 servings | 60 min | 270 kcal

- Red bell peppers, 4 medium ≈ 600 g
- Quinoa, 120 g (≈ 3/4 cup)
- Onion, 1 medium ≈ 150 g
- Garlic, 2 cloves
- Tomatoes, 400 g
- Black beans (canned), 400 g
- Corn kernels (canned), 150 g
- Olive oil, 1 tablespoon ≈ 15 ml
- Ground cumin, 1 teaspoon ≈ 2 g
- Paprika, 1 teaspoon ≈ 2 g
- Black pepper, 1/2 teaspoon ≈ 1 g
- Fresh cilantro, 10 g
- Lime, 1 medium ≈ 70 g
- No salt

PREPARATION 10 min:

Preheat the oven to 180°C (350°F). Cook the quinoa according to package instructions. Cut the tops off the bell peppers and remove the seeds. Dice the onion. Mince the garlic. Dice the fresh tomatoes into small cubes. Chop the fresh cilantro. Squeeze the lime juice.

COOKING 50 min:

Heat olive oil in a large skillet over medium heat. Sauté onion and garlic until soft (about 5 min). Add cooked quinoa, diced fresh tomatoes, black beans, corn, cumin, paprika, and black pepper. Cook for 5 minutes, stirring occasionally. Off heat, stir in cilantro and lime juice. Stuff bell peppers with quinoa mixture, place in baking dish, cover with foil. Bake in preheated oven for 25-30 minutes, until peppers are tender and filling is hot.

CAL	270 kcal	SODIUM	40 mg
CARBS	45 g	POTASSIUM	750 mg
PROTEIN	9 g	CALCIUM	70 g
FAT	9 g	MAGNESIUM	80 g

per serving

GARLIC-LEMON SHRIMP SKEWERS

4 servings | 30 min | 150 kcal

- Large shrimp, 400 g
- Olive oil, 2 tablespoons ≈ 30 ml
- Fresh lemon juice, 2 tbsp ≈ 30 ml
- Lemon zest, 1 tsp ≈ 2 g
- Garlic, 4 cloves
- Fresh parsley, 2 tbsp ≈ 10 g
- Ground black pepper, 1/2 tsp ≈ 1 g
- Wooden skewers, soaked in water for 30 minutes
- No salt

PREPARATION 15 min:

Peel and mince the garlic. In a bowl, combine olive oil, lemon juice, zest, garlic, parsley, and pepper. Peel the shrimp if needed. Add to the marinade and mix well. Marinate for 15 minutes.

COOKING 10 min:

Preheat the grill to medium-high heat. Thread the marinated shrimp onto the soaked wooden skewers. Grill the shrimp skewers for about 2-3 minutes per side, until the shrimp are opaque and cooked through.

ASSEMBLY 5 min:

Remove the shrimp from the grill and let it rest for a couple of minutes. Serve hot, garnished with additional fresh parsley and lemon wedges if desired.

CAL	150 kcal	SODIUM	105 mg
CARBS	3 g	POTASSIUM	220 mg
PROTEIN	20 g	CALCIUM	80 g
FAT	7 g	MAGNESIUM	40 g

per serving

TOFU STIR-FRY WITH VEGETABLES

4 servings | 35 min | 220 kcal

- Firm tofu, 400 g
- Broccoli florets, 200 g
- Carrot, 2 medium ≈ 140 g
- Red bell pepper, 1 large ≈ 180 g
- Snow peas, 100 g
- Onion, 1 medium ≈ 150 g
- Garlic, 3 cloves
- Fresh ginger, 1 tablespoon ≈ 15 g
- Olive oil, 2 tablespoons ≈ 30 ml
- Low-sodium soy sauce, 2 tablespoons ≈ 30 ml
- Rice vinegar, 1 tablespoon ≈ 15 ml
- Sesame oil, 1 teaspoon ≈ 5 ml
- Cornstarch, 1 tablespoon ≈ 10 g
- Water, 2 tablespoons ≈ 30 ml
- Fresh cilantro, chopped, 2 tablespoons ≈ 10 g
- Black pepper, a pinch
- No salt

PREPARATION 15 min:

Press tofu to extract water, then cube it. Mince garlic and ginger. Peel and slice carrots, and cut broccoli into florets. Slice red bell pepper and onion. Combine cornstarch with water.

COOKING 20 min:

Heat olive oil in a skillet, fry tofu until golden, remove. Add garlic and ginger, sauté, then include all vegetables, cooking for 5-7 minutes until crisp-tender. Return tofu, add soy sauce, rice vinegar, sesame oil, and cornstarch mixture. Cook for 2-3 minutes until sauce thickens. Garnish with cilantro and black pepper. Serve hot.

CAL	220 kcal	SODIUM	200 mg
CARBS	20 g	POTASSIUM	600 mg
PROTEIN	12 g	CALCIUM	150 mg
FAT	12 g	MAGNESIUM	60 g

per serving

LENTIL AND VEGETABLE SHEPHERD'S PIE

4 servings | 90 min | 350 kcal

- Green or brown lentils, 200 g
- Carrots, 2 medium, ≈ 140 g
- Celery, 2 stalks, ≈ 80 g
- Onion, 1 medium, ≈ 150 g
- Garlic, 3 cloves
- Mushrooms, 200 g
- Tomato paste, 2 tablespoons ≈ 30 g
- Low-sodium vegetable broth, 480 ml
- Olive oil, 2 tablespoons ≈ 30 ml
- Fresh thyme, 2 sprigs
- Fresh rosemary, 1 sprig
- Potatoes, 600 g
- Low-fat milk, 120 ml
- Fresh parsley, chopped, 2 tablespoons ≈ 10 g
- Ground black pepper, a pinch
- No salt

PREPARATION 20 min:

Dice the potatoes, carrots, and onion. Chop the celery and mushrooms. Mince the garlic. Rinse the lentils.

COOKING 70 min:

Boil the potatoes until tender, about 15 minutes. Sauté the onion, carrot, celery, garlic, and mushrooms in olive oil until soft, about 10 minutes. Add the lentils, tomato paste, broth, thyme, rosemary, and black pepper. Simmer for 20-25 minutes, then remove the herbs. Mash the boiled potatoes with milk and olive oil until smooth, and stir in the black pepper and parsley. Heat the oven to 200°C (400°F). In a baking dish, layer the lentil mix, top with the mashed potatoes, and bake for 15-20 minutes until golden.

CAL	350 kcal	SODIUM	70 mg
CARBS	60 g	POTASSIUM	950 mg
PROTEIN	12 g	CALCIUM	100 g
FAT	8 g	MAGNESIUM	60 g

per serving

GRILLED TURKEY BURGERS

4 servings | 40 min | 360 kcal

For the Burgers:
- Ground turkey (lean), 500 g
- Onion, 1 small, ≈ 70 g
- Garlic, 2 cloves
- Fresh parsley, 2 tbsp ≈ 10 g
- Olive oil, 1 tbsp ≈ 15 ml
- Fresh lemon juice, 1 tbsp ≈ 15 ml
- Ground black pepper, 1/2 tsp ≈ 1 g
- Salt, a pinch
- Whole wheat burger buns, 4
- Toppings (tomatoes, cucumbers, greens)

For the Avocado Yogurt Sauce:
- Avocado, 1 medium ≈ 150 g
- Low-fat plain yogurt, 120 ml
- Fresh lime juice, 1 tbsp ≈ 15 ml
- Garlic, 1 clove
- Fresh cilantro, chopped, 1 tbsp ≈ 5 g
- Ground black pepper, a pinch

PREPARATION 20 min:

Peel and chop the onion and garlic. In a bowl, mix ground turkey, onion, garlic, parsley, olive oil, lemon juice, pepper, and salt. Form the mixture into 4 patties. For the sauce, peel the avocado and remove the pit. Blend the avocado, yogurt, lime juice, garlic, cilantro, and pepper until smooth.

COOKING 20 min:

Preheat the grill to medium-high heat. Grill patties for 6-7 minutes per side until cooked. Spread sauce on buns, add patties, top with more sauce. Add optional toppings. Serve hot.

CAL	360 kcal	SODIUM	130 mg
CARBS	30 g	POTASSIUM	650 mg
PROTEIN	30 g	CALCIUM	80 g
FAT	15 g	MAGNESIUM	40 g

per serving

BAKED COD WITH TOMATOES

4 servings | 40 min | 200 kcal

- Cod fillets, 4 pieces, ≈ 600 g
- Cherry tomatoes, 200 g
- Olive oil, 2 tbsp ≈ 30 ml
- Garlic, 3 cloves
- Fresh parsley, 2 tbsp ≈ 10 g
- Fresh lemon juice, 2 tbsp ≈ 30 ml
- Ground black pepper, 1/2 tsp ≈ 1 g
- No salt

PREPARATION 10 min:

Preheat the oven to 200°C (400°F). Peel and mince the garlic. Halve the cherry tomatoes. In a small bowl, combine olive oil, lemon juice, minced garlic, and black pepper.

COOKING 25 min:

Place the cod fillets in a baking dish. Scatter the halved cherry tomatoes around the fillets. Pour the olive oil mixture over the fish and vegetables. Bake for 20-25 minutes, until the cod is opaque and flakes easily with a fork.

ASSEMBLY 5 min:

Remove the baking dish from the oven. Sprinkle the chopped fresh parsley over the top. Serve hot, optionally garnished with additional lemon wedges.

CAL	200 kcal	SODIUM	60 mg
CARBS	6 g	POTASSIUM	750 mg
PROTEIN	28 g	CALCIUM	40 g
FAT	9 g	MAGNESIUM	40 g

per serving

VG

BLACK BEAN AND SWEET POTATO ENCHILADAS

4 servings | 1,5 hour | 350 kcal

- Sweet potatoes, 2 medium ≈ 400 g
- Black beans (canned), 240 g
- Corn tortillas, 8 small
- Red bell pepper, 1 medium ≈ 150 g
- Red onion, 1/2 medium ≈ 50 g
- Garlic, 2 cloves
- Olive oil, 2 tablespoons ≈ 30 ml
- Cumin, 1 teaspoon ≈ 2 g
- Chili powder, 1 teaspoon ≈ 2 g
- Fresh cilantro, 10 g
- Lime juice, 2 tablespoons ≈ 30 ml
- Tomato sauce (no salt), 240 ml
- Black pepper, a pinch. No salt

PREPARATION 30 min

Drain and rinse the black beans. Dice sweet potatoes, bell pepper, and onion. Mince garlic. Chop cilantro.

For the sauce, heat 1 tablespoon of olive oil in a pan and cook 1 minced garlic clove for 1-2 minutes. Add tomato sauce, 1/2 teaspoon cumin, 1/2 teaspoon chili powder, and black pepper. Simmer for 10 minutes. Preheat the oven to 180°C (350°F).

COOKING 60 min:

Heat 1 tablespoon of olive oil in a skillet. Cook sweet potatoes for 10 minutes. Add bell pepper, onion, and garlic; cook for 5 minutes. Add beans, cumin, chili powder, and black pepper; cook for 5 minutes. Remove from heat, stir in cilantro and lime juice. Spread some tomato sauce in a baking dish. Fill tortillas with sweet potato mixture, roll up, and place seam-side down. Top with remaining sauce, drizzle with olive oil. Bake for 20 minutes until tortillas are crisp.

CAL	350 kcal	SODIUM	40 mg
CARBS	58 g	POTASSIUM	750 mg
PROTEIN	8 g	CALCIUM	70 mg
FAT	10 g	MAGNESIUM	70 g

per serving

CHICKEN AND VEGETABLE KABOBS

4 servings | 40 min | 220 kcal

- Chicken breast: 400g
- Red bell pepper: 1 large ≈ 180g
- Yellow bell pepper: 1 large ≈ 180g
- Zucchini: 1 medium ≈ 200g
- Red onion: 1 medium ≈ 150g
- Olive oil: 2 tbsp ≈ 30ml
- Lemon juice: 2 tbsp ≈ 30ml
- Garlic: 3 cloves
- Chopped rosemary: 1 tbsp ≈ 5g
- Chopped thyme: 1 tbsp ≈ 5g
- Ground black pepper: 1/2 tsp ≈ 1g
- Soaked wooden skewers
- No salt

PREPARATION 20 min:

Cut chicken into bite-sized pieces, chop bell peppers, zucchini, and onion to similar sizes. Mince garlic.

Mix olive oil, lemon juice, garlic, rosemary, thyme, and pepper in a bowl, add chicken and veggies, marinate 30 min.

COOKING 15 min:

Heat grill to medium-high. Thread chicken and veggies onto skewers. Grill 12-15 min, turning occasionally, until chicken is cooked and veggies are tender.

ASSEMBLY 5 min:

Remove kabobs from grill, let rest, and serve hot, optionally garnished with fresh herbs.

CAL	220 kcal	SODIUM	70 mg
CARBS	10 g	POTASSIUM	550 mg
PROTEIN	28 g	CALCIUM	30 g
FAT	9 g	MAGNESIUM	25 g

per serving

STUFFED ZUCCHINI BOATS

4 servings | 1,1 hour | 200 kcal

- Zucchini, 4 medium ≈ 600 g
- Quinoa, 120 g (1/2 cup)
- Black beans (canned, drained, and rinsed), 240 g (1 cup)
- Cherry tomatoes, 150 g
- Red onion, 1/2 medium ≈ 50 g
- Garlic, 2 cloves
- Olive oil, 2 tablespoons ≈ 30 ml
- Cumin, 1 teaspoon ≈ 2 g
- Chili powder, 1 teaspoon ≈ 2 g
- Fresh cilantro, 10 g
- Lime juice, 2 tablespoons ≈ 30 ml
- Black pepper, a pinch
- Salt, a pinch

PREPARATION 20 min:

Collect ingredients, rinse and prepare zucchini, cherry tomatoes, and cilantro. Hollow out zucchini halves, dice insides. Cook quinoa, dice tomatoes, chop onion, garlic, and cilantro.

COOKING 50 min:

Heat the oven to 180°C (350°F). Sauté the zucchini flesh, onion, and garlic in olive oil until soft. Mix in the quinoa, black beans, tomatoes, cumin, chili powder, black pepper, and salt. Cook for 5 minutes, then add the cilantro and lime juice. Arrange the zucchini boats on a baking sheet, drizzle with olive oil, and fill them with the quinoa mixture. Bake for 20 minutes until the zucchini is tender and the filling is hot.

CAL	200 kcal	SODIUM	120 mg
CARBS	30 g	POTASSIUM	600 mg
PROTEIN	6 g	CALCIUM	40 g
FAT	7 g	MAGNESIUM	50 g

per serving

GINGER-SOY GLAZED TOFU

4 servings | 40 min | 170 kcal

- Firm tofu, 400 g
- Fresh ginger, 1 tablespoon ≈ 15 g
- Garlic, 2 cloves
- Soy sauce (low-sodium), 60 ml ≈ 1/4 cup
- Maple syrup, 2 tablespoons ≈ 30 ml
- Rice vinegar, 1 tablespoon ≈ 15 ml
- Sesame oil, 1 tablespoon ≈ 15 ml
- Cornstarch, 1 tablespoon ≈ 8 g
- Green onions, 10 g
- Sesame seeds, 1 tablespoon ≈ 10 g
- Black pepper, a pinch
- No salt

PREPARATION 15 min:

Collect ingredients. Press and cube tofu. Grate ginger, mince garlic, and chop green onions.

COOKING 20 min:

Whisk together ginger, garlic, soy sauce, maple syrup, rice vinegar, sesame oil, and pepper in a bowl. In another bowl, toss the tofu cubes in cornstarch. Cook the tofu in a non-stick skillet over medium heat until golden and crispy, about 8-10 minutes, then set it aside. Add the ginger-soy mixture to the skillet, simmer until slightly thickened, about 2-3 minutes. Return the tofu to the skillet, toss with the sauce, and cook another 2-3 minutes until glazed.

ASSEMBLY 5 min:

Transfer the glazed tofu to a serving dish. Garnish with chopped green onions and sesame seeds.

CAL	170 kcal	SODIUM	200 mg
CARBS	15 g	POTASSIUM	250 mg
PROTEIN	10 g	CALCIUM	150 g
FAT	8 g	MAGNESIUM	40 g

per serving

HERB-CRUSTED TILAPIA

4 servings | 50 min | 180 kcal

- Tilapia fillets, 4 ≈ 600 g
- Fresh parsley, 20 g
- Fresh dill, 20 g
- Fresh thyme, 10 g
- Lemon zest, 1 tablespoon ≈ 6 g
- Garlic, 2 cloves
- Olive oil, 2 tablespoons ≈ 30 ml
- Black pepper, a pinch
- No salt

PREPARATION 15 min:

Gather all ingredients. Rinse the fresh herbs and finely chop them. Zest the lemon. Mince the garlic.

COOKING 20 min:

Preheat the oven to 200°C (400°F). In a small bowl, mix the chopped parsley, dill, thyme, lemon zest, minced garlic, black pepper, and 1 tablespoon of olive oil to form the herb mixture. Place the tilapia fillets on a baking sheet lined with parchment paper, skin-side down. Brush each fillet with the remaining tablespoon of olive oil. Evenly distribute the herb mixture over the top of each fillet, pressing down gently to adhere.

BAKING 15 min:

Bake in the preheated oven for 12-15 minutes, or until the fish is opaque and flakes easily with a fork.

CAL	180 kcal	SODIUM	80 mg
CARBS	2 g	POTASSIUM	500 mg
PROTEIN	30 g	CALCIUM	40 mg
FAT	6 g	MAGNESIUM	30 g

per serving

EGGPLANT PARMESAN WITH WHOLE WHEAT BREADCRUMBS

4 servings | 1,25 hour | 350 kcal

- Eggplant, 2 medium ≈ 500 g
- Whole wheat breadcrumbs, 120 g
- Parmesan cheese, grated, 60 g
- Mozzarella cheese, part-skim, 240 g (2 cups)
- Marinara sauce (no salt added), 480 ml (2 cups)
- Olive oil, 2 tablespoons ≈ 30 ml
- Fresh basil, 10 g
- Fresh parsley, 10 g
- Garlic powder, 1 teaspoon ≈ 2 g
- Black pepper, a pinch. No salt

PREPARATION 20 min:

Gather all ingredients. Rinse the eggplants and slice them into 1 cm (1/2 inch) thick rounds. Finely chop the fresh basil and parsley.

COOKING 65 min:

Preheat the oven to 200°C (400°F). Line a baking sheet with parchment, brush with olive oil. Arrange the eggplant slices in a single layer, brush with olive oil, and sprinkle with black pepper. Bake for 20 minutes, flipping once, until tender and golden. In a dish, mix the breadcrumbs, Parmesan, garlic powder, and black pepper. Coat the eggplant slices in the breadcrumb mixture by pressing firmly. In a baking dish (approximately 9x13 inches), spread 1/2 cup of marinara sauce on the bottom. Add a layer of breaded eggplant slices, and top with 1/2 cup of mozzarella. Repeat the layers, ending with marinara and mozzarella on top. Bake for 20 minutes until the cheese is bubbly and golden. Garnish with fresh basil and parsley.

CAL	350 kcal	SODIUM	200 mg
CARBS	30 g	POTASSIUM	790 mg
PROTEIN	20 g	CALCIUM	350 g
FAT	18 g	MAGNESIUM	50 g

per serving

SPAGHETTI SQUASH WITH MARINARA AND TURKEY MEATBALLS

4 servings | 1,1 hour | 320 kcal

- Spaghetti squash, 1 large ≈ 1200 g
- Ground turkey, 400 g
- Egg, 1 large
- Whole wheat breadcrumbs, 60 g
- Fresh parsley, 10 g
- Garlic powder, 1 teaspoon ≈ 2 g
- Onion powder, 1 teaspoon ≈ 2 g
- Black pepper, a pinch
- Olive oil, 2 tablespoons ≈ 30 ml
- Marinara sauce (no salt), 480 ml
- Fresh basil, 10 g
- Fresh oregano, 5 g
- Parmesan cheese optional ≈ 30 g
- No salt

PREPARATION 20 min:

Gather ingredients. Preheat oven to 200°C (400°F). Halve the spaghetti squash and remove seeds. Brush with olive oil and place cut-side down on a parchment-lined baking sheet.

COOKING 50 min:

Bake the squash for 35-40 minutes until tender. While baking, mix turkey, egg, breadcrumbs, parsley, garlic powder, onion powder, and black pepper to form 1-inch meatballs. Brown the meatballs in olive oil in a skillet for about 10 minutes, then set aside. Simmer marinara sauce in the same skillet, return the meatballs, and cook for 5 more minutes.

Scrape the flesh of the baked spaghetti squash into strands using a fork and place in a serving bowl. Top with marinara, meatballs, and optional basil, oregano, and Parmesan.

CAL	320 kcal	SODIUM	80 mg
CARBS	25 g	POTASSIUM	800 mg
PROTEIN	24 g	CALCIUM	70 g
FAT	14 g	MAGNESIUM	60 g

per serving

ZUCCHINI NOODLES WITH PESTO AND GRILLED CHICKEN

4 servings | 40 min | 300 kcal

- Zucchini, 4 medium ≈ 600 g
- Chicken breast, 400 g
- Olive oil, 2 tbsp ≈ 30 ml
- Fresh basil leaves, 30 g
- Pine nuts, 30 g
- Garlic, 2 cloves
- Lemon juice, 2 tbsp ≈ 30 ml
- Nutritional yeast, 2 tbsp (optional)
- Black pepper, a pinch
- No salt

PREPARATION 15 min:

Gather all ingredients. Rinse the zucchini and basil leaves. Spiralize the zucchini to create zucchini noodles. Mince the garlic.

COOKING 20 min:

Preheat the grill to medium-high. Brush the chicken with olive oil, season with black pepper, and grill for 6-7 minutes on each side until cooked. Let the chicken rest, then slice it. Meanwhile, blend the basil, pine nuts, garlic, lemon juice, nutritional yeast (if using), and olive oil into pesto in a food processor. Sauté the zucchini noodles for 2-3 minutes until al dente.

ASSEMBLY 5 min:

Toss the zucchini noodles with pesto, place on plates, and top with the sliced chicken. Optionally garnish with basil or pine nuts.

CAL	300 kcal	SODIUM	70 mg
CARBS	10 g	POTASSIUM	900 mg
PROTEIN	28 g	CALCIUM	50 g
FAT	18 g	MAGNESIUM	60 g

per serving

PAN-SEARED RED FISH WITH LEMON-HONEY GLAZE

2 servings | **22 min** | **350 kcal**

- Red fish fillets (e.g., salmon or trout), 2 pieces ≈ 300 g each
- Olive oil, 1 tablespoon ≈ 15 ml
- Lemon juice, 2 tablespoons ≈ 30 ml
- Honey, 1 teaspoon ≈ 5 ml
- Mixed herbs for fish (e.g., dill, parsley, thyme), 1 teaspoon ≈ 1 g
- Black pepper, 1/2 teaspoon ≈ 1 g

PREPARATION 5 min:

Pat the red fish fillets dry with paper towels. Sprinkle the mixed herbs and black pepper evenly over both sides of the fish.

COOKING 15 min:

Heat olive oil in a non-stick skillet over medium heat. Sear fish fillets for 2.5-3 minutes each side until golden, then set aside. Add lemon juice and honey to the skillet, stirring to combine. Simmer gently, return fish to skillet, and spoon the glaze over it. Cover and simmer on low for 2.5 minutes, flip the fish, and continue to simmer for another 2.5 minutes.

ASSEMBLY 2 min:

Remove the fish from the skillet and serve hot, drizzling any remaining glaze over the top.

CAL	350 kcal	SODIUM	105 mg
CARBS	8 g	POTASSIUM	830 mg
PROTEIN	40 g	CALCIUM	50 mg
FAT	18 g	MAGNESIUM	50 g

per serving

BROILED SEA BASS WITH CITRUS SALSA

4 servings | **35 min** | **220 kcal**

- Sea bass fillets, 4 ≈ 600 g
- Orange, 1 large ≈ 180 g
- Grapefruit, 1 large ≈ 230 g
- Lime, 1 medium ≈ 70 g
- Red onion, 1/2 medium ≈ 50 g
- Fresh cilantro, 10 g
- Jalapeño, 1 small ≈ 15 g (optional)
- Olive oil, 1 tablespoon ≈ 15 ml
- Black pepper, a pinch
- No salt

PREPARATION 15 min:

Gather all ingredients. Peel and segment the orange and grapefruit, then cut the segments into small pieces. Juice the lime. Finely chop the red onion, cilantro, and jalapeño (if using).

COOKING 15 min:

Preheat the oven to 230°C (450°F) and set it to broil. Line a broiler pan with foil and lightly brush with olive oil. Place the sea bass fillets on the prepared pan and brush them with olive oil. Season with black pepper. Broil the sea bass fillets for about 8-10 minutes, or until the fish is opaque and flakes easily with a fork.

ASSEMBLY 5 min:

While the fish is broiling, combine the orange, grapefruit, red onion, cilantro, and jalapeño (if using) in a bowl. Add the lime juice and mix well to create the citrus salsa. Serve the broiled sea bass fillets topped with the fresh citrus salsa.

CAL	220 kcal	SODIUM	80 mg
CARBS	10 g	POTASSIUM	650 mg
PROTEIN	28 g	CALCIUM	50 mg
FAT	9 g	MAGNESIUM	45 g

per serving

CHICKPEA AND SPINACH CURRY

4 servings | 40 min | 260 kcal

- Chickpeas (canned, drained, and rinsed), 480 g (2 cups)
- Fresh spinach, 200 g
- Coconut milk (unsweetened), 400 ml (1 can)
- Onion, 1 medium ≈ 100 g
- Garlic, 3 cloves
- Fresh ginger, 1 tablespoon ≈ 15 g
- Tomato paste, 2 tablespoons ≈ 30 g
- Olive oil, 1 tablespoon ≈ 15 ml
- Ground cumin, 1 teaspoon ≈ 2 g
- Ground coriander, 1 teaspoon ≈ 2 g
- Ground turmeric, 1 teaspoon ≈ 2 g
- Ground paprika, 1 teaspoon ≈ 2 g
- Garam masala, 1 teaspoon ≈ 2 g
- Black pepper, a pinch
- Fresh cilantro, 10 g
- Lime juice, 1 tablespoon ≈ 15 ml
- No salt

PREPARATION 10 min:

Gather all the ingredients. Finely chop the onion, garlic, and ginger. Rinse and drain the chickpeas, rinse the fresh spinach, and chop the fresh cilantro.

COOKING 30 min:

Heat olive oil in a large pot over medium heat. Add chopped onion, garlic, and ginger, and sauté for 5 minutes. Stir in spices and cook for 2 minutes. Add tomato paste and cook for 1 minute. Pour in coconut milk and simmer for 5 minutes. Add drained chickpeas and fresh spinach, and cook for 5-7 minutes until spinach wilts and chickpeas are heated through. Stir in lime juice and chopped cilantro. Serve over brown rice or with whole wheat naan bread.

VG

CAL	260 kcal	SODIUM	45 mg
CARBS	28 g	POTASSIUM	700 mg
PROTEIN	8 g	CALCIUM	80 g
FAT	13 g	MAGNESIUM	80 g

per serving

MEDITERRANEAN QUINOA WITH SAUTÉED SHRIMP

4 servings | 50 min | 320 kcal

- Quinoa, 180 g (1 cup)
- Water, 360 ml (1.5 cups)
- Shrimp, peeled and deveined, 400 g
- Cucumber, 1 medium ≈ 150 g
- Cherry tomatoes, 200 g
- Red onion, 1/2 medium ≈ 50 g
- Kalamata olives 50 g (1/4 cup)
- Fresh parsley, 10 g
- Fresh mint, 10 g
- Olive oil, 3 tablespoons ≈ 45 ml
- Lemon juice, 2 tablespoons ≈ 30 ml
- Garlic, 2 cloves
- Dried oregano, 1 teaspoon ≈ 1 g
- Black pepper, a pinch
- No salt

PREPARATION 20 min:

Gather ingredients. Rinse quinoa, cucumber, cherry tomatoes, parsley, and mint. Chop cucumber, tomatoes, parsley, and mint. Finely chop red onion and mince garlic.

COOKING 20 min:

Boil water in a medium saucepan. Add quinoa, reduce heat, cover, and simmer for 15 minutes until tender. Let cool. Preheat grill. Toss shrimp with olive oil, garlic, oregano, and black pepper. Grill shrimp for 2-3 minutes per side until cooked.

ASSEMBLY 10 min:

Combine cooked quinoa, cucumber, tomatoes, red onion, olives, parsley, and mint in a large bowl. Whisk olive oil and lemon juice in a small bowl. Pour dressing over salad and toss. Top with grilled shrimp and serve.

CAL	320 kcal	SODIUM	150 mg
CARBS	25 g	POTASSIUM	600 mg
PROTEIN	20 g	CALCIUM	80 g
FAT	15 g	MAGNESIUM	70 g

per serving

VEGETABLE PAELLA WITH SAFFRON

4 servings | 65 min | 350 kcal

- Whole grain rice, 300 g (1.5 cups)
- Vegetable broth (no salt added), 720 ml (3 cups)
- Saffron threads, 1/2 teaspoon ≈ 1 g
- Olive oil, 2 tablespoons ≈ 30 ml
- Onion, 1 medium ≈ 100 g
- Garlic, 3 cloves
- Red bell pepper, 1 medium ≈ 150 g
- Yellow bell pepper, 1 medium ≈ 150 g
- Zucchini, 1 medium ≈ 200 g
- Cherry tomatoes, 200 g
- Green beans, 150 g
- Peas, 100 g
- Smoked paprika, 1 teaspoon ≈ 2 g
- Ground turmeric, 1 teaspoon ≈ 2 g
- Black pepper, a pinch
- Fresh parsley, 10 g
- Lemon wedges, for serving
- No salt

PREPARATION 20 min:

Gather ingredients. Finely chop onion and garlic. Rinse and chop bell peppers, zucchini, and green beans. Halve cherry tomatoes. Chop parsley.

COOKING 45 min:

Heat olive oil in a large pan. Sauté onion and garlic for 5 minutes. Add bell peppers, zucchini, and green beans, and cook for 5 minutes. Stir in Arborio rice, paprika, turmeric, and pepper. Cook for 2 minutes. Add saffron to broth, pour into pan. Simmer for 15 minutes. Add tomatoes and peas, cook for 10-15 minutes until rice is tender and liquid absorbed. Remove from heat, cover, and let rest for 5 minutes. Sprinkle with parsley and serve with lemon wedges.

CAL	350 kcal	SODIUM	40 mg
CARBS	60 g	POTASSIUM	600 mg
PROTEIN	8 g	CALCIUM	50 mg
FAT	9 g	MAGNESIUM	40 g

per serving

BAKED LEMON GARLIC TOFU

4 servings | 55+ min | 160 kcal

- Firm tofu, 400 g
- Lemon juice, 3 tablespoons ≈ 45 ml
- Lemon zest, 1 teaspoon ≈ 2 g
- Garlic, 4 cloves
- Olive oil, 2 tablespoons ≈ 30 ml
- Black pepper, a pinch
- Fresh parsley, 10 g
- No salt

PREPARATION 20 min + marinate:

Gather all ingredients. Press the tofu to remove excess moisture, then cut it into bite-sized cubes. Mince the garlic. Finely chop the fresh parsley. Whisk lemon juice, zest, minced garlic, olive oil, and black pepper in a bowl. Toss tofu cubes in mixture. Marinate for 30 minutes.

COOKING 30 min:

Preheat the oven to 200°C (400°F). Line a baking sheet with parchment paper. Arrange the marinated tofu cubes in a single layer on the baking sheet. Bake for 25-30 minutes, or until the tofu is golden brown and slightly crispy, flipping halfway through.

ASSEMBLY 5 min:

Remove the tofu from the oven and let it cool slightly. Transfer to a serving dish and garnish with chopped fresh parsley.

CAL	160 kcal	SODIUM	10 mg
CARBS	5 g	POTASSIUM	150 mg
PROTEIN	10 g	CALCIUM	200 g
FAT	12 g	MAGNESIUM	30 g

per serving

GRILLED FISH TACOS WITH MANGO SALSA

4 servings | 45 min | 260 kcal

For the Fish Tacos:
- White fish fillets (e.g., tilapia, cod), 400 g
- Olive oil, 2 tablespoons ≈ 30 ml
- Lime juice, 2 tablespoons ≈ 30 ml
- Ground cumin, 1 teaspoon ≈ 2 g
- Ground paprika, 1 teaspoon ≈ 2 g
- Garlic powder, 1 teaspoon ≈ 2 g
- Black pepper, a pinch
- Corn tortillas, 8 small
- Fresh cilantro, 10 g

For the Mango Salsa:
- Mango, 1 large ≈ 200 g
- Red bell pepper, 1 medium ≈ 150 g
- Red onion, 1/4 medium ≈ 25 g
- Jalapeño, 1 small ≈ 15 g (optional)
- Fresh cilantro, 10 g
- Lime juice, 2 tablespoons ≈ 30 ml
- Black pepper, a pinch. **No salt**

PREPARATION 20 min:

Gather ingredients. Rinse and dry fish fillets. Mix olive oil, lime juice, cumin, paprika, garlic powder, and black pepper in a bowl. Marinate fish for 15 minutes. Finely chop red bell pepper, red onion, jalapeño (if using), and cilantro. Peel and dice mango.

COOKING 25 min:

Preheat grill to medium-high. Grill fish for 3-4 minutes per side until opaque and flaky. Let rest, then flake into pieces. In a bowl, combine mango, bell pepper, onion, jalapeño, cilantro, lime juice, and black pepper for salsa. Warm tortillas on grill for 1 minute each side. Fill tortillas with fish and top with salsa. Garnish with cilantro.

CAL	260 kcal	SODIUM	60 mg
CARBS	25 g	POTASSIUM	600 mg
PROTEIN	20 g	CALCIUM	60 g
FAT	10 g	MAGNESIUM	40 g

per serving

BARLEY RISOTTO WITH MUSHROOMS

4 servings | 50 min | 300 kcal

- Pearl barley: 200g (1 cup)
- Mushrooms: 300g
- Vegetable broth: 1 liter (4 cups)
- Olive oil: 2 tbsp (30ml)
- Onion: 1 medium (100g)
- Garlic: 3 cloves
- White wine: 120ml (1/2 cup)
- Parmesan cheese, grated: 40g
- Fresh parsley: 10g
- Black pepper: a pinch
- Salt: a pinch

PREPARATION 15 min:

Gather ingredients. Finely chop onion and garlic. Clean and slice mushrooms. Chop parsley.

COOKING 45 min:

Heat 1 tbsp olive oil in a large pan over medium heat. Sauté onion and garlic until translucent, about 5 minutes. Add mushrooms and cook until browned, about 8 minutes. Stir in pearl barley and cook for 2 minutes. Add white wine and cook until absorbed. Gradually add vegetable broth, one cup at a time, stirring until absorbed each time. Cook until barley is tender and creamy, about 30 minutes.

ASSEMBLY 5 min:

Stir in Parmesan, parsley, remaining olive oil, salt, and pepper. Mix well and adjust seasoning.

CAL	300 kcal	SODIUM	180 mg
CARBS	48 g	POTASSIUM	450 mg
PROTEIN	10 g	CALCIUM	70 g
FAT	9 g	MAGNESIUM	50 g

per serving

GREEK CHICKEN SOUVLAKI

4 servings | 40+ min | 240 kcal

- Chicken breast, boneless and skinless, 600 g
- Olive oil, 3 tablespoons ≈ 45 ml
- Lemon juice, 2 tablespoons ≈ 30 ml
- Garlic, 3 cloves
- Fresh oregano, 2 tablespoons ≈ 10 g
- Fresh parsley, 1 tablespoon ≈ 5 g
- Black pepper, 1/2 teaspoon ≈ 1 g
- Wooden skewers, soaked in water for 30 minutes

PREPARATION 20 min + marinate:

Gather all ingredients. Rinse the chicken breasts and cut them into bite-sized cubes. Mince the garlic and finely chop the fresh oregano and parsley.
In a large bowl, combine the olive oil, lemon juice, minced garlic, chopped oregano, parsley, and black pepper. Add the chicken cubes to the bowl and toss to coat evenly. Cover and refrigerate for at least 1 hour to marinate.

COOKING 45 min:

Preheat the grill to medium-high heat. Thread the marinated chicken cubes onto the soaked wooden skewers. Grill the chicken skewers for about 10-12 minutes, turning occasionally, until the chicken is cooked through and has a nice char.

ASSEMBLY 5 min:

Serve the chicken souvlaki with a side of Greek salad, pita bread, and Lemon Herb Yogurt Dressing p.97.

CAL	240 kcal	SODIUM	70 mg
CARBS	2 g	POTASSIUM	450 mg
PROTEIN	28 g	CALCIUM	30 mg
FAT	14 g	MAGNESIUM	35 g

per serving

VG

THAI BASIL TOFU

4 servings | 50 min | 210 kcal

- Firm tofu, 400 g
- Fresh basil leaves, 30 g
- Red bell pepper, 1 medium ≈ 150 g
- Green bell pepper, 1 medium ≈ 150 g
- Carrot, 1 medium ≈ 60 g
- Onion, 1 medium ≈ 100 g
- Garlic, 3 cloves
- Fresh ginger, 1 tablespoon ≈ 15 g
- Olive oil, 2 tablespoons ≈ 30 ml
- Soy sauce (low-sodium), 60 ml (1/4 cup)
- Lime juice, 1 tablespoon ≈ 15 ml
- Agave syrup or maple syrup, 1 tablespoon ≈ 15 ml
- Cornstarch, 1 tablespoon ≈ 8 g
- Water, 2 tablespoons ≈ 30 ml
- Black pepper, a pinch
- No salt

PREPARATION 20 min:

Gather ingredients. Press and cube tofu. Thinly slice bell peppers, carrot, and onion. Mince garlic, grate ginger, and rinse basil leaves.

COOKING 30 min:

Heat 1 tbsp olive oil in a skillet or wok over medium-high. Cook tofu until crispy, 8-10 minutes, set aside. In the same skillet, heat remaining oil, sauté garlic and ginger for 1 minute. Add onion, bell peppers, and carrot, stir-fry for 5-7 minutes. Mix soy sauce, lime juice, agave syrup, cornstarch, and water in a bowl. Pour into skillet, cook until sauce thickens, about 2 minutes. Return tofu to skillet, toss with sauce and vegetables. Add basil leaves, stir until wilted, about 1 minute. Season with pepper. Serve over rice or quinoa.

CAL	210 kcal	SODIUM	240 mg
CARBS	16 g	POTASSIUM	450 mg
PROTEIN	12 g	CALCIUM	200 g
FAT	12 g	MAGNESIUM	30 g

per serving

BUTTERNUT SQUASH AND BLACK BEAN CHILI

4 servings | 1,1 hour | 250 kcal

- Butternut squash: 1 medium (900g)
- Black beans (canned, drained, rinsed): 400g
- Diced tomatoes (canned): 400g
- Red bell pepper: 1 medium (150g)
- Onion: 1 medium (150g)
- Garlic: 3 cloves
- Olive oil: 1 tbsp (15ml)
- Chili powder: 2 tbsp (14g)
- Cumin: 1 tbsp (8g)
- Smoked paprika: 1 tsp (2g)
- Black pepper: 1/2 tsp (1g)
- Cayenne pepper: 1/4 tsp (0.5g)
- Fresh cilantro: 10g
- Lime: 1 medium (70g)
- Carrot: 1 medium (60g)
- Celery stalks: 2 (100g)
- Bay leaf: 1
- No salt

PREPARATION 15 min:

Peel and dice butternut squash, red bell pepper, and onion. Mince garlic. Drain and rinse black beans. Chop cilantro, carrot, and celery.

COOKING 60 min:

Combine carrot, celery, bay leaf, and 1.5 liters of water in a pot. Boil, then simmer for 30 minutes to make broth. Strain and set aside. In a large pot, heat olive oil over medium heat. Sauté onion and garlic until soft (5 min). Add squash and bell pepper, cook for 5 min. Stir in chili powder, cumin, smoked paprika, black pepper, and cayenne for 1 min. Add broth and tomatoes, bring to a boil. Simmer for 20 min until squash is tender. Add black beans, cook for 10 min. Squeeze lime juice into chili, stir. Serve hot

CAL	250 kcal	SODIUM	150 mg
CARBS	45 g	POTASSIUM	800 mg
PROTEIN	8 g	CALCIUM	100 g
FAT	6 g	MAGNESIUM	70 g

per serving

SESAME-CRUSTED AHI TUNA

2 servings | 30 min | 370 kcal

- Ahi tuna steaks: 2 (300g each)
- Black sesame seeds: 2 tbsp (20g)
- White sesame seeds: 2 tbsp (20g)
- Olive oil: 1 tbsp (15ml)
- Low-sodium soy sauce: 1 tbsp (15ml)
- Fresh ginger: 1 tsp (5g)
- Garlic: 2 cloves
- Lime: 1 medium (70g)
- Green onions: 2 stalks (30g)
- Avocado: 1 medium (150g)
- No salt

PREPARATION 15 min:

Mince the garlic and ginger. Squeeze the lime juice. Finely chop the green onions. Slice the avocado.

COOKING 10 min:

In a shallow dish, combine the low-sodium soy sauce, minced garlic, minced ginger, and lime juice. Marinate the ahi tuna steaks in this mixture for 5 minutes on each side. While the tuna is marinating, mix the black and white sesame seeds on a plate. Remove the tuna from the marinade and press both sides into the sesame seeds to coat. Heat the olive oil in a non-stick skillet over medium-high heat. Sear the tuna steaks for 1-2 minutes on each side for rare, or 3-4 minutes for medium, depending on your preference.

ASSEMBLY 5 min:

Slice the seared tuna steaks and arrange them on a serving plate. Garnish with chopped green onions and avocado slices. Serve immediately.

CAL	370 kcal	SODIUM	160 mg
CARBS	8 g	POTASSIUM	800 mg
PROTEIN	37 g	CALCIUM	200 g
FAT	22 g	MAGNESIUM	90 g

per serving

CHICKEN STIR-FRY WITH BROCCOLI AND CARROTS

4 servings | 40 min | 240 kcal

- Skinless, boneless chicken breast, 300 g
- Broccoli florets, 200 g
- Carrots, 2 medium ≈ 120 g
- Red bell pepper, 1 medium ≈ 150 g
- Green onions, 2 stalks ≈ 30 g
- Garlic, 2 cloves
- Fresh ginger, 1 teaspoon ≈ 5 g
- Olive oil, 1 tablespoon ≈ 15 ml
- Low-sodium soy sauce, 2 tablespoons ≈ 30 ml
- Sesame oil, 1 teaspoon ≈ 5 ml
- Black pepper, 1/2 teaspoon ≈ 1 g
- No salt

PREPARATION 15 min:

Cut chicken breast into thin strips. Chop broccoli florets. Peel and slice carrots. Slice the red bell pepper. Mince garlic and ginger. Chop green onions.

COOKING 20 min:

Heat olive oil in a large skillet or wok over medium-high. Cook chicken until browned and cooked through (5-7 min), then set aside. In the same skillet, sauté garlic and ginger for 1 min. Add broccoli, carrots, and bell pepper, stir-fry for 5-7 min until tender-crisp. Return chicken to skillet. Add soy sauce, sesame oil, and black pepper. Stir and cook for 2-3 min until heated through.

ASSEMBLY 5 min:

Transfer to a serving dish, garnish with green onions. Serve immediately.

CAL	240 kcal	SODIUM	70 mg
CARBS	2 g	POTASSIUM	450 mg
PROTEIN	28 g	CALCIUM	30 mg
FAT	14 g	MAGNESIUM	35 g

per serving

LEMON GARLIC SHRIMP WITH ASPARAGUS

4 servings | 30 min | 200 kcal

- Large shrimp (peeled), 400 g
- Asparagus, 300 g
- Olive oil, 2 tablespoons ≈ 30 ml
- Garlic, 3 cloves
- Lemon juice, 3 tablespoons ≈ 45 ml
- Lemon zest, 1 teaspoon ≈ 2 g
- Black pepper, 1/2 teaspoon ≈ 1 g
- Fresh parsley, 10 g
- No salt

PREPARATION 10 min:

Mince the garlic. Chop the fresh parsley. Zest and juice the lemon.

COOKING 15 min:

Heat 1 tablespoon of olive oil in a large skillet over medium heat. Add the asparagus and cook for 3-4 minutes until tender but still crisp. Remove from the skillet and set aside. In the same skillet, add the remaining olive oil and minced garlic, cooking until fragrant (≈ 1 min). Add the shrimp, lemon juice, lemon zest, and black pepper. Cook for 2-3 minutes on each side until the shrimp are pink and opaque.

ASSEMBLY 5 min:

Return the cooked asparagus to the skillet with the shrimp and toss to combine. Garnish with chopped fresh parsley and serve immediately.

CAL	200 kcal	SODIUM	170 mg
CARBS	5 g	POTASSIUM	400 mg
PROTEIN	28 g	CALCIUM	70 g
FAT	8 g	MAGNESIUM	35 g

per serving

SIDE DISHES

GOOD FOOD CHOICES ARE GOOD INVESTMENTS

LEMON GARLIC ROASTED CAULIFLOWER

4 servings | 40 min | 80 kcal

- Cauliflower, 1 large head ≈ 600 g
- Olive oil, 2 tablespoons ≈ 30 ml
- Lemon juice, 2 tablespoons ≈ 30 ml
- Garlic, 4 cloves ≈ 12 g
- Black pepper, 1/4 teaspoon ≈ 1 g
- Fresh parsley, chopped, 2 tablespoons ≈ 8 g

PREPARATION 10 min:

Preheat your oven to 200°C (392°F). Wash the cauliflower and cut it into florets. Peel and finely chop the garlic.

COOKING 25 min:

In a large bowl, combine the olive oil, lemon juice, chopped garlic, and black pepper. Add the cauliflower florets to the bowl and toss well to coat them evenly with the mixture. Spread the cauliflower florets on a baking sheet in a single layer. Roast in the preheated oven for 25 minutes, or until the cauliflower is golden brown and tender.

ASSEMBLY 5 min:

Remove the roasted cauliflower from the oven and transfer it to a serving dish. Sprinkle with chopped fresh parsley before serving.

CAL	80 kcal	SODIUM	15 mg
CARBS	8 g	POTASSIUM	320 mg
PROTEIN	2 g	CALCIUM	30 mg
FAT	5 g	MAGNESIUM	15 g

per serving

STEAMED GREEN BEANS WITH LEMON

4 servings | 20 min | 50 kcal

- Fresh green beans, 400 g
- Lemon juice, 1 tablespoon ≈ 15 ml
- Olive oil, 1 tablespoon ≈ 15 ml
- Fresh dill, 1 tablespoon ≈ 4 g
- Black pepper, 1/4 teaspoon ≈ 1 g
- No salt

PREPARATION 5 min:

Wash the green beans and trim the ends.

COOKING 10 min:

Fill a pot with a few inches of water and bring it to a boil. Place the green beans in a steamer basket over the boiling water, cover, and steam for 5-7 minutes until the beans are tender but still crisp. Remove the beans from the steamer and transfer them to a serving bowl.

ASSEMBLY 5 min:

In a small bowl, mix the lemon juice and olive oil. Drizzle this mixture over the steamed green beans. Sprinkle with chopped fresh dill and black pepper. Toss gently to combine and serve immediately.

CAL	50 kcal	SODIUM	10 mg
CARBS	7 g	POTASSIUM	190 mg
PROTEIN	1,5 g	CALCIUM	40 g
FAT	2,5 g	MAGNESIUM	15 g

per serving

MASHED CAULIFLOWER WITH CHIVES

4 servings | 1,1 hour | 70 kcal

- Cauliflower, 1 large head ≈ 600 g
- Unsweetened almond milk, 1/4 cup ≈ 60 ml
- Olive oil, 2 tablespoons ≈ 30 ml
- Garlic, 2 cloves ≈ 6 g
- Fresh chives, chopped, 2 tablespoons ≈ 8 g
- Black pepper, 1/4 teaspoon ≈ 1 g
- No salt

PREPARATION 10 min:

Wash the cauliflower and cut it into florets. Peel and chop the garlic. Chop the fresh chives.

COOKING 15 min:

Bring a large pot of water to a boil. Add the cauliflower florets and cook for 10-12 minutes until tender. Drain the cauliflower and transfer it to a food processor. Add the almond milk, olive oil, and garlic. Blend until smooth and creamy.

ASSEMBLY 5 min:

Transfer the mashed cauliflower to a serving bowl. Stir in the chopped chives and black pepper. Serve warm.

CAL	70 kcal	SODIUM	15 mg
CARBS	7 g	POTASSIUM	320 mg
PROTEIN	2 g	CALCIUM	40 g
FAT	4,5 g	MAGNESIUM	15 g

per serving

QUINOA PILAF WITH VEGETABLES

4 servings | 35 min | 190 kcal

- Quinoa, 1 cup ≈ 185 g
- Water, 2 cups ≈ 480 ml
- Olive oil, 2 tablespoons ≈ 30 ml
- Carrot, 1 medium ≈ 60 g
- Red bell pepper, 1 medium ≈ 120 g
- Zucchini, 1 medium ≈ 200 g
- Green peas, 1/2 cup ≈ 75 g
- Garlic, 2 cloves ≈ 6 g
- Fresh parsley, chopped, 2 tablespoons ≈ 8 g
- Black pepper, 1/4 teaspoon ≈ 1 g
- No salt

PREPARATION 10 min:

Rinse the quinoa under cold water. Peel and dice the carrot. Dice the red bell pepper and zucchini. Mince the garlic.

COOKING 20 min:

In a medium pot, bring the water to a boil. Add the quinoa, reduce the heat to low, cover, and simmer for about 15 minutes, or until the water is absorbed and the quinoa is tender. In a large pan, heat the olive oil over medium heat. Add the garlic and sauté for about 1 minute until fragrant. Add the diced carrot, red bell pepper, and zucchini to the pan. Cook for about 5 minutes, stirring occasionally, until the vegetables are tender. Stir in the green peas and cook for another 2-3 minutes.

ASSEMBLY 5 min:

Add the cooked quinoa to the pan with the vegetables and mix well. Stir in the chopped parsley and black pepper. Serve warm.

CAL	190 kcal	SODIUM	10 mg
CARBS	28 g	POTASSIUM	350 mg
PROTEIN	5 g	CALCIUM	30 g
FAT	6 g	MAGNESIUM	60 g

per serving

HONEY ROASTED CARROTS WITH GARLIC AND THYME

2 servings | 45 min | 130 kcal

- Carrots, 450 g
- Olive oil, 1.5 tablespoons ≈ 22.5 ml
- Honey, 1 tablespoon ≈ 15 ml
- Garlic, minced, 2 large cloves
- Dried thyme, 1 teaspoon ≈ 2 g
- Black pepper, to taste
- Lemon juice, 1/4 lemon ≈ 7.5 ml
- Fresh parsley, chopped, 1/2 tablespoon ≈ 2 g

PREPARATION 10 min:

Preheat the oven to 205°C (400°F). Peel the carrots and chop into 1.5-2 inch pieces.

COOKING 30 min:

In a large baking dish or lined baking sheet, mix carrots with olive oil, honey, garlic, thyme, and black pepper until evenly coated. Roast for 30-45 minutes, tossing halfway through.

ASSEMBLY 5 min:

Remove from oven, toss with lemon juice and parsley. Optionally drizzle with extra honey and season with additional black pepper if desired. Serve hot.

CAL	130 kcal	SODIUM	20 mg
CARBS	21 g	POTASSIUM	380 mg
PROTEIN	1 g	CALCIUM	40 mg
FAT	5 g	MAGNESIUM	15 g

per serving

SWEET POTATO WEDGES WITH PAPRIKA

4 servings | 45 min | 140 kcal

- Sweet potatoes, 600 g
- Olive oil, 2 tablespoons ≈ 30 ml
- Paprika, 1 teaspoon ≈ 2 g
- Garlic powder, 1/2 teaspoon ≈ 1 g
- Black pepper, 1/4 teaspoon ≈ 1 g
- Fresh parsley, 1 tablespoon ≈ 4 g
- No salt

PREPARATION 10 min:

Preheat your oven to 200°C (392°F). Wash the sweet potatoes and cut them into wedges.

COOKING 30 min:

In a large bowl, toss the sweet potato wedges with olive oil, paprika, garlic powder, and black pepper until evenly coated. Arrange the wedges in a single layer on a baking sheet. Roast in the preheated oven for 25-30 minutes, turning halfway through, until the sweet potatoes are tender and golden brown.

ASSEMBLY 5 min:

Transfer the roasted sweet potato wedges to a serving dish. Sprinkle with chopped fresh parsley before serving.

CAL	140 kcal	SODIUM	20 mg
CARBS	22 g	POTASSIUM	440 mg
PROTEIN	1,5 g	CALCIUM	30 g
FAT	5 g	MAGNESIUM	20 g

per serving

BROWN RICE WITH HERBS

4 servings | 50 min | 150 kcal

- Brown rice, 1 cup ≈ 185 g
- Water, 2 cups ≈ 480 ml
- Olive oil, 1 tbsp ≈ 15 ml
- Fresh parsley, 2 tbsp ≈ 8 g
- Fresh basil, 1 tbsp ≈ 4 g
- Fresh thyme, 1 tbsp ≈ 4 g
- Garlic, 2 cloves ≈ 6 g
- Lemon zest, 1 tsp ≈ 2 g
- Black pepper, 1/4 tsp ≈ 1 g
- No salt

PREPARATION 5 min:

Rinse the brown rice under cold water. Peel and mince the garlic. Chop the fresh parsley, basil, and thyme.

COOKING 40 min:

In a medium pot, bring the water to a boil. Add the rinsed brown rice, reduce the heat to low, cover, and simmer for about 40 minutes, or until the water is absorbed and the rice is tender. In a small pan, heat the olive oil over medium heat. Add the minced garlic and sauté for about 1 minute until fragrant.

ASSEMBLY 5 min:

Once the rice is cooked, fluff it with a fork and transfer it to a large bowl. Add the sautéed garlic, chopped herbs, lemon zest, and black pepper. Mix well to combine. Serve warm.

CAL	150 kcal	SODIUM	10 mg
CARBS	28 g	POTASSIUM	150 mg
PROTEIN	3 g	CALCIUM	20 g
FAT	4 g	MAGNESIUM	50 g

per serving

BALSAMIC GLAZED ROASTED BEETS

4 servings | 60 min | 80 kcal

- Beets, 4 medium ≈ 500 g
- Balsamic vinegar, 2 tbsp ≈ 30 ml
- Olive oil, 1 tbsp ≈ 15 ml
- Fresh thyme, 1 tbsp ≈ 4 g
- Black pepper, 1/4 tsp ≈ 1 g
- No salt

PREPARATION 10 min:

Preheat your oven to 200°C (392°F). Wash and peel the beets. Cut them into wedges.

COOKING 45 min:

In a large bowl, toss the beet wedges with olive oil and black pepper until evenly coated. Spread the beets in a single layer on a baking sheet. Roast in the preheated oven for 35-40 minutes, or until the beets are tender and slightly caramelized, stirring halfway through cooking. In the last 5 minutes of roasting, drizzle the balsamic vinegar over the beets and toss to coat. Return to the oven for the final 5 minutes.

ASSEMBLY 5 min:

Transfer the roasted beets to a serving dish. Sprinkle with fresh thyme before serving. Serve warm or at room temperature.

CAL	80 kcal	SODIUM	15 mg
CARBS	13 g	POTASSIUM	320 mg
PROTEIN	1,5 g	CALCIUM	20 g
FAT	3,5 g	MAGNESIUM	20 g

per serving

SAUTÉED SPINACH WITH GARLIC

4 servings | 11 min | 45 kcal

- Fresh spinach, 400 g
- Olive oil, 1 tablespoon ≈ 15 ml
- Garlic, 4 cloves ≈ 12 g
- Lemon juice, 1 tablespoon ≈ 15 ml
- Lemon zest, 1 teaspoon ≈ 2 g
- Black pepper, 1/4 teaspoon ≈ 1 g
- No salt

PREPARATION 5 min:

Wash the spinach thoroughly and drain well. Peel and thinly slice the garlic. Zest and juice the lemon.

COOKING 5 min:

In a large pan, heat the olive oil over medium heat. Add the sliced garlic and sauté for about 1 minute until fragrant and slightly golden. Add the spinach to the pan in batches, stirring constantly, until wilted. This should take about 3-4 minutes. Add the lemon juice, lemon zest, and black pepper, and stir well.

ASSEMBLY 1 min:

Transfer the sautéed spinach to a serving dish. Serve immediately.

CAL	45 kcal	SODIUM	30 mg
CARBS	5 g	POTASSIUM	470 mg
PROTEIN	2 g	CALCIUM	80 mg
FAT	3 g	MAGNESIUM	70 g

per serving

BROCCOLI WITH LEMON ZEST

4 servings | 17 min | 60 kcal

- Broccoli, 500 g
- Olive oil, 1 tablespoon ≈ 15 ml
- Lemon zest, 1 tablespoon ≈ 6 g
- Garlic, 2 cloves ≈ 6 g
- Black pepper, 1/4 teaspoon ≈ 1 g
- No salt

PREPARATION 5 min:

Wash the broccoli and cut it into florets. Peel and mince the garlic. Zest the lemon.

COOKING 10 min:

Bring a large pot of water to a boil. Add the broccoli florets and blanch for 2-3 minutes until bright green and slightly tender. Drain the broccoli and set aside. In a large pan, heat the olive oil over medium heat. Add the minced garlic and sauté for about 1 minute until fragrant. Add the blanched broccoli to the pan and sauté for an additional 3-4 minutes until tender.

ASSEMBLY 2 min:

Transfer the sautéed broccoli to a serving dish. Sprinkle with lemon zest and black pepper. Serve immediately.

CAL	60 kcal	SODIUM	20 mg
CARBS	7 g	POTASSIUM	340 mg
PROTEIN	3 g	CALCIUM	40 g
FAT	3 g	MAGNESIUM	20 g

per serving

CAULIFLOWER RICE WITH PARSLEY

4 servings | 22 min | 55 kcal

- Cauliflower, 1 medium head ≈ 600 g
- Olive oil, 1 tablespoon ≈ 15 ml
- Fresh parsley, chopped, 2 tablespoons ≈ 8 g
- Garlic, 2 cloves ≈ 6 g
- Lemon juice, 1 tablespoon ≈ 15 ml
- Black pepper, 1/4 teaspoon ≈ 1 g
- No salt

PREPARATION 10 min:

Wash and chop the cauliflower into florets. Use a food processor to pulse the cauliflower until it resembles rice. Peel and mince the garlic. Chop the fresh parsley.

COOKING 10 min:

In a large pan, heat the olive oil over medium heat. Add the minced garlic and sauté for about 1 minute until fragrant. Add the cauliflower rice to the pan and cook, stirring frequently, for about 5-7 minutes until the cauliflower is tender but not mushy.

ASSEMBLY 2 min:

Remove the pan from the heat and stir in the lemon juice, chopped parsley, and black pepper. Mix well to combine. Transfer the cauliflower rice to a serving dish. Serve warm.

CAL	55 kcal	SODIUM	20 mg
CARBS	7 g	POTASSIUM	320 mg
PROTEIN	2 g	CALCIUM	30 g
FAT	3 g	MAGNESIUM	15 g

per serving

GRILLED ASPARAGUS WITH OLIVE OIL

4 servings | 16 min | 50 kcal

- Asparagus, 500 g
- Olive oil, 1 tbsp ≈ 15 ml
- Lemon zest, 1 tsp ≈ 2 g
- Black pepper, 1/4 tsp ≈ 1 g
- No salt

PREPARATION 5 min:

Wash the asparagus and trim the woody ends. Zest the lemon.

COOKING 10 min:

Preheat the grill to medium-high. Toss asparagus with olive oil and black pepper. Grill for 5-7 minutes, turning occasionally, until tender and slightly charred.

ASSEMBLY 1 min:

Transfer to a serving dish. Sprinkle with lemon zest. Serve immediately.

CAL	50 kcal	SODIUM	10 mg
CARBS	4 g	POTASSIUM	230 mg
PROTEIN	2 g	CALCIUM	30 g
FAT	3,5 g	MAGNESIUM	15 g

per serving

WILD RICE WITH MUSHROOMS

4 servings | 60 min | 180 kcal

- Wild rice, 1 cup ≈ 185 g
- Water, 3 cups ≈ 720 ml
- Olive oil, 1 tbsp ≈ 15 ml
- Mushrooms, 250 g
- Onion, 1 medium ≈ 110 g
- Garlic, 2 cloves ≈ 6 g
- Fresh parsley, 2 tbsp ≈ 8 g
- Black pepper, 1/4 tsp ≈ 1 g
- No salt

PREPARATION 10 min:

Rinse the wild rice. Wash and slice the mushrooms. Dice the onion. Mince the garlic. Cut the parsley.

COOKING 45 min:

Bring water to a boil in a pot. Add wild rice, reduce heat, cover, and simmer for 40-45 minutes until tender. In a large pan, heat olive oil over medium heat. Sauté onion for 3 minutes. Add garlic and sauté for 1 minute. Add mushrooms and cook for 5-7 minutes until golden.

ASSEMBLY 5 min:

Add cooked rice to the pan. Stir to combine. Season with black pepper and mix in parsley. Transfer to a serving dish. Serve warm.

CAL	180 kcal	SODIUM	15 mg
CARBS	32 g	POTASSIUM	350 mg
PROTEIN	5 g	CALCIUM	20 mg
FAT	4 g	MAGNESIUM	45 g

per serving

WHOLE WHEAT SPAGHETTI WITH CHERRY TOMATOES

4 servings | 35 min | 230 kcal

- Whole wheat spaghetti, 250 g
- Cherry tomatoes, 2 cups ≈ 300 g
- Olive oil, 2 tbsp ≈ 30 ml
- Garlic, 4 cloves ≈ 12 g
- Fresh basil, 1/4 cup ≈ 10 g
- Black pepper, 1/4 tsp ≈ 1 g
- Lemon juice, 1 tbsp ≈ 15 ml
- Red pepper flakes, 1/4 tsp ≈ 1 g (optional)
- No salt

PREPARATION 10 min:

Wash and halve the cherry tomatoes. Peel and thinly slice the garlic. Chop the basil.

COOKING 20 min:

Bring a pot of water to a boil. Cook spaghetti until al dente, 9-11 minutes. Drain and reserve 1/4 cup of pasta water. In a pan, heat olive oil over medium heat. Sauté garlic for 1-2 minutes until fragrant and golden. Add tomatoes and cook for 5-7 minutes until softened. Add red pepper flakes, if using.

ASSEMBLY 5 min:

Add spaghetti to the pan. Toss, adding pasta water if needed. Stir in lemon juice, basil, and black pepper. Mix well. Serve immediately.

CAL	230 kcal	SODIUM	10 mg
CARBS	38 g	POTASSIUM	400 mg
PROTEIN	7 g	CALCIUM	40 g
FAT	7 g	MAGNESIUM	50 g

per serving

DESSERTS

STRESSED IS DESSERTS SPELLED
BACKWARDS

VG

BAKED APPLES WITH CINNAMON AND WALNUTS

4 portions | **42 min** | **180 kcal**

- Apples, 4 medium ≈ 600 g
- Walnuts, chopped, 1/4 cup ≈ 30 g
- Raisins, 1/4 cup ≈ 40 g
- Ground cinnamon, 1 tsp ≈ 2 g
- Maple syrup, 2 tbsp ≈ 30 ml
- Lemon juice, 1 tbsp ≈ 15 ml

PREPARATION 10 min:

Preheat oven to 175°C (350°F). Wash and core apples to create a hollow center.

COOKING 30 min:

Mix walnuts, raisins, cinnamon, and maple syrup in a bowl. Stuff apples with the mixture. Place apples in a baking dish, drizzle with lemon juice. Cover with foil and bake for 25-30 minutes until tender.

ASSEMBLY 2 min:

Let apples cool slightly before serving. Transfer to a serving dish and serve warm.

CAL	180 kcal	SODIUM	5 mg
CARBS	34 g	POTASSIUM	250 mg
PROTEIN	2 g	CALCIUM	20 mg
FAT	6 g	MAGNESIUM	25 g

per serving

VT

BAKED PEARS WITH HONEY AND ALMONDS

4 portions | **40 min** | **120 kcal**

- Pears, 4 medium ≈ 600 g
- Honey, 2 tbsp ≈ 30 ml
- Sliced almonds, 2 tbsp ≈ 16 g
- Ground cinnamon, 1/2 tsp ≈ 1.2 g
- Low-fat plain yogurt, 120 ml
- Lemon juice, 1 tbsp ≈ 15 ml

PREPARATION 10 min:

Preheat the oven to 180°C (350°F). Wash the pears and cut them in half. Remove the cores. Place the pear halves in a baking dish.

COOKING 25 min:

Drizzle the pears with honey and sprinkle with ground cinnamon. Bake in the preheated oven for 20-25 minutes, until tender.

ASSEMBLY 5 min:

Remove the pears from the oven and let them cool slightly. Top each pear half with a spoonful of yogurt, a sprinkle of sliced almonds, and a drizzle of lemon juice.

CAL	120 kcal	SODIUM	20 mg
CARBS	28 g	POTASSIUM	220 mg
PROTEIN	2 g	CALCIUM	50 g
FAT	2 g	MAGNESIUM	15 g

per serving

STRAWBERRIES AND CREAM

2 portions | **15 min** | **120 kcal**

- Fresh strawberries, 300 g
- Low-fat plain Greek yogurt, 240 ml
- Honey, 1 tablespoon ≈ 15 ml
- Vanilla extract, 1 teaspoon ≈ 5 ml
- Fresh mint leaves, for garnish (optional)

PREPARATION 10 min:

Wash the strawberries thoroughly and remove the stems. Cut the strawberries into halves or quarters, depending on their size. In a small bowl, mix the low-fat plain Greek yogurt with honey and vanilla extract until smooth and well combined.

ASSEMBLY 5 min:

In serving bowls or glasses, layer the cut strawberries. Spoon the yogurt mixture over the strawberries. Garnish with fresh mint leaves if desired.

CAL	120 kcal	SODIUM	40 mg
CARBS	21 g	POTASSIUM	400 mg
PROTEIN	6 g	CALCIUM	150 g
FAT	2 g	MAGNESIUM	25 g

per serving

DARK CHOCOLATE AVOCADO MOUSSE

4 portions | **30 min** | **220 kcal**

- Ripe avocados, 2 medium ≈ 300 g
- Dark chocolate (70% cocoa or higher), 100 g
- Unsweetened cocoa powder, 2 tablespoons ≈ 10 g
- Maple syrup, 2 tablespoons ≈ 30 ml
- Vanilla extract, 1 teaspoon ≈ 5 ml
- Almond milk (unsweetened), 2 tablespoons ≈ 30 ml

PREPARATION 10 min:

Melt the dark chocolate in a heatproof bowl over a pot of simmering water (double boiler method) or in the microwave in short bursts, stirring until smooth. Let it cool slightly.

COOKING 15 min:

Peel and pit the avocados. Place the avocado flesh in a food processor. Add the melted dark chocolate, cocoa powder, maple syrup, vanilla extract, and almond milk. Blend until smooth and creamy.

ASSEMBLY 5 min:

Transfer the mousse into serving bowls or glasses. Chill in the refrigerator for at least 1 hour before serving.

CAL	220 kcal	SODIUM	10 mg
CARBS	23 g	POTASSIUM	500 mg
PROTEIN	3 g	CALCIUM	30 g
FAT	15 g	MAGNESIUM	60 g

per serving

VG

FRESH FRUIT SALAD WITH MINT

4 portions 20 min 90 kcal

- Strawberries, 1 cup ≈ 150 g
- Blueberries, 1 cup ≈ 150 g
- Kiwi, 2 medium ≈ 140 g
- Orange, 1 large ≈ 180 g
- Grapes, 1 cup ≈ 150 g
- Fresh mint, chopped, 2 tbsp ≈ 8 g
- Lemon juice, 1 tbsp ≈ 15 ml

PREPARATION 15 min:

Wash all the fruits thoroughly. Hull and slice the strawberries. Peel and slice the kiwi. Peel and segment the orange. Halve the grapes if desired. Chop the fresh mint.

ASSEMBLY 5 min:

In a large bowl, combine all the prepared fruits. Drizzle with lemon juice and gently toss to combine. Sprinkle with chopped mint and mix well. Serve immediately or chill in the refrigerator for 10-15 minutes before serving.

CAL	90 kcal	SODIUM	5 mg
CARBS	22 g	POTASSIUM	250 mg
PROTEIN	1,5 g	CALCIUM	40 mg
FAT	0,5 g	MAGNESIUM	15 g

per serving

VT

ALMOND BUTTER COOKIES

12 cookies 40 min 130 kcal

- Almond butter, 1 cup ≈ 240 g
- Honey, 1/4 cup ≈ 85 g
- Whole wheat flour, 1/2 cup ≈ 60 g
- Baking powder, 1 tsp ≈ 4 g
- Vanilla extract, 1 tsp ≈ 5 ml
- Almond milk (unsweetened), 2 tbsp ≈ 30 ml
- Ground flaxseed, 1 tbsp ≈ 7 g
- No salt

PREPARATION 10 min:

Preheat oven to 175°C (350°F). Line a baking sheet with parchment paper. Mix ground flaxseed with 3 tbsp of water, let sit for 5 minutes.

COOKING 25 min:

In a large bowl, combine almond butter, honey, and vanilla extract. Mix well. Add thickened flaxseed mixture and almond milk, stir until incorporated. In a separate bowl, whisk whole wheat flour and baking powder. Gradually add to wet mixture, stirring until dough forms. Scoop tablespoon-sized portions of dough onto baking sheet, flatten with a fork. Bake for 12-15 minutes until edges are golden brown.

ASSEMBLY 5 min:

Let cookies cool on the baking sheet for a few minutes, then transfer to a wire rack to cool completely. Serve once cooled.

CAL	130 kcal	SODIUM	20 mg
CARBS	10 g	POTASSIUM	100 mg
PROTEIN	3 g	CALCIUM	40 g
FAT	9 g	MAGNESIUM	30 g

per serving

LEMON RICOTTA CHEESECAKE

8 portions | **1.25 h** | **280 kcal**

- Ricotta cheese (low-fat), 500 g
- Cream cheese (low-fat), 250 g
- Honey, 1/2 cup ≈ 170 g
- Eggs, 3 large ≈ 150 g
- Lemon zest, 2 tbsp ≈ 12g
- Lemon juice, 1/4 cup ≈ 60ml
- Vanilla extract, 1 tsp ≈ 5ml
- Whole wheat graham crackers, 1 cup ≈ 120 g
- Almonds, finely chopped, 1/4 cup ≈ 30 g
- Unsalted butter, melted, 3 tbsp ≈ 45ml

PREPARATION 20 min:

Preheat oven to 175°C (350°F). Grease a 9-inch springform pan. Crush the graham crackers in a food processor. Mix the crushed graham crackers with almonds and melted butter. Press mixture into the pan to form a crust. Set aside.

COOKING 60 min:

In a large bowl, beat ricotta cheese, cream cheese, and honey until smooth. Add eggs one at a time, beating well. Stir in lemon zest, lemon juice, and vanilla extract. Pour mixture over crust and smooth the top. Bake for 50-60 minutes until the center is set and edges are lightly golden. Let cool to room temperature.

ASSEMBLY 5 min:

Refrigerate cheesecake for at least 4 hours or overnight. Remove from springform pan and transfer to a serving plate. Slice and serve.

CAL	280 kcal	SODIUM	160 mg
CARBS	22 g	POTASSIUM	180 mg
PROTEIN	12 g	CALCIUM	200 mg
FAT	17 g	MAGNESIUM	20 g

per serving

BANANA OATMEAL COOKIES

12 cookies | **30 min** | **90 kcal**

- Ripe bananas, 2 medium ≈ 240 g
- Rolled oats, 1 1/2 cups ≈ 150 g
- Almond butter, 1/4 cup ≈ 60 g
- Honey, 2 tbsp ≈ 30 g
- Vanilla extract, 1 tsp ≈ 5 ml
- Ground cinnamon, 1 tsp ≈ 2 g
- Baking powder, 1/2 tsp ≈ 2 g
- Dark chocolate chips (optional), 1/4 cup ≈ 40 g

PREPARATION 10 min:

Preheat oven to 175°C (350°F). Line a baking sheet with parchment paper. Mash ripe bananas in a large bowl until smooth.

COOKING 15 min:

Add almond butter, honey, and vanilla extract to mashed bananas, mix well. In a separate bowl, combine rolled oats, ground cinnamon, and baking powder. Gradually add dry ingredients to wet mixture, stirring until combined. Fold in dark chocolate chips if using. Scoop tablespoon-sized portions of dough onto baking sheet, flattening each cookie slightly. Bake for 12-15 minutes until golden brown and set.

ASSEMBLY 5 min:

Let cookies cool on the baking sheet for a few minutes, then transfer to a wire rack to cool completely. Serve once cooled.

CAL	90 kcal	SODIUM	5 mg
CARBS	15 g	POTASSIUM	115 mg
PROTEIN	2 g	CALCIUM	15 g
FAT	3 g	MAGNESIUM	20 g

per serving

STRAWBERRY BANANA SORBET

4 portions | 20 min | 80 kcal

- Strawberries, hulled, 2 cups ≈ 300 g
- Ripe bananas, 2 medium ≈ 240 g
- Lemon juice, 1 tablespoon ≈ 15 ml
- Honey, 2 tablespoons ≈ 30 ml (optional)

PREPARATION 10 min:

Wash and hull the strawberries. Slice the ripe bananas. Place the strawberries and banana slices on a baking sheet lined with parchment paper and freeze for at least 2 hours, or until completely frozen.

BLENDING 5 min:

Once the fruits are frozen, transfer them to a food processor or high-speed blender. Add the lemon juice and honey (or agave syrup for a vegan option). Blend until the mixture is smooth and creamy, scraping down the sides as needed.

ASSEMBLY 5 min:

Scoop the sorbet into bowls or cups and serve immediately for a soft-serve texture. Alternatively, transfer the sorbet to an airtight container and freeze for an additional 1-2 hours for a firmer texture. Then scoop and serve.

CAL	80 kcal	SODIUM	1 mg
CARBS	20 g	POTASSIUM	240 mg
PROTEIN	1 g	CALCIUM	15 mg
FAT	0,5 g	MAGNESIUM	15 g

per serving

BLUEBERRY ALMOND CRUMBLE

6 portions | 40 min | 180 kcal

- Fresh blueberries, 4 cups ≈ 600 g
- Lemon juice, 1 tbsp ≈ 15 ml
- Honey, 2 tbsp ≈ 30 ml
- Almond flour, 1 cup ≈ 120 g
- Rolled oats, 1/2 cup ≈ 50 g
- Sliced almonds, 1/4 cup ≈ 30 g
- Coconut oil (melted), 1/4 cup ≈ 60 ml
- Ground cinnamon, 1 tsp ≈ 2 g
- Vanilla extract, 1 tsp ≈ 5 ml

PREPARATION 10 min:

Preheat the oven to 175°C (350°F). In a small bowl, mix the lemon juice and 1 tablespoon of honey until well combined. Pour this mixture over the blueberries in a larger bowl and gently mix until the blueberries are evenly coated. Then spread the blueberry mixture evenly in a baking dish.

MIXING AND COOKING 40 min:

In a medium bowl, combine the almond flour, rolled oats, sliced almonds, melted coconut oil, ground cinnamon, vanilla extract, and the remaining tablespoon of honey. Mix everything together until the mixture becomes crumbly. Sprinkle this crumbly mixture evenly over the blueberries in the baking dish. Bake for 25-30 minutes until golden and bubbly.

ASSEMBLY 5 min:

Let cool slightly before serving. Serve warm with dairy-free yogurt or vanilla almond milk ice cream.

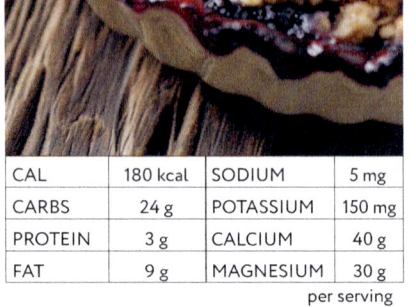

CAL	180 kcal	SODIUM	5 mg
CARBS	24 g	POTASSIUM	150 mg
PROTEIN	3 g	CALCIUM	40 g
FAT	9 g	MAGNESIUM	30 g

per serving

MANGO COCONUT TAPIOCA

4 portions | 35 min | 180 kcal

- Tapioca pearls, 100 g
- Light coconut milk, 400 ml
- Water, 500 ml
- Mango, diced, 1 medium ≈ 200 g
- Honey, 2 tablespoons ≈ 30 ml
- Vanilla extract, 1 teaspoon ≈ 5 ml
- Fresh mint leaves, for garnish (optional)

PREPARATION 10 min:

Gather all the ingredients. Dice the mango into small cubes.

COOKING 20 min:

In a medium saucepan, bring water to a boil. Add tapioca pearls and cook for about 10 minutes, stirring frequently until the pearls become translucent. Drain and rinse under cold water to remove excess starch. In another saucepan, combine the coconut milk, honey, and vanilla extract. Bring to a gentle simmer over medium heat. Add the cooked tapioca pearls to the coconut milk mixture and cook for an additional 5 minutes, stirring frequently.

ASSEMBLY 5 min:

Divide the tapioca mixture into serving bowls. Top with diced mango and garnish with fresh mint leaves, if desired. Serve warm or chilled.

CAL	180 kcal	SODIUM	15 mg
CARBS	31 g	POTASSIUM	160 mg
PROTEIN	1 g	CALCIUM	20 g
FAT	5 g	MAGNESIUM	15 g

per serving

RASPBERRY CHIA JAM

10 portions | 20 min | 33 kcal

- Fresh raspberries, 250 g
- Chia seeds, 2 tablespoons ≈ 30 g
- Honey, 2 tablespoons ≈ 30 ml
- Lemon juice, 1 tablespoon ≈ 15 ml
- Water, 2 tablespoons ≈ 30 ml

PREPARATION 5 min:

Gather all ingredients. Wash the raspberries.

COOKING 10 min:

In a medium saucepan, combine the raspberries and water. Cook over medium heat, stirring occasionally, until the raspberries start to break down and become syrupy, about 5 minutes. Mash the raspberries with a fork or a potato masher to your desired consistency.

ASSEMBLY 5 min:

Remove the saucepan from heat and stir in the chia seeds, honey, and lemon juice. Mix well until all the ingredients are combined. Let the mixture sit for about 5 minutes to allow the chia seeds to thicken the jam. Transfer the jam to a clean jar and let it cool completely before refrigerating. Store in the refrigerator for up to two weeks.

CAL	33 kcal	SODIUM	1 mg
CARBS	5 g	POTASSIUM	45 mg
PROTEIN	0,5 g	CALCIUM	15 g
FAT	0,5 g	MAGNESIUM	5 g

per serving

APPLE CINNAMON BITES

12 portions | **55 min** | **110 kcal**

- Rolled oats, 150 g
- Unsweetened applesauce, 120 ml
- Apple, 1 medium ≈ 180 g
- Almond butter, 2 tbsp ≈ 30 g
- Honey, 2 tbsp ≈ 30 ml
- Ground cinnamon, 1 tsp ≈ 3 g
- Vanilla extract, 1 tsp ≈ 5 ml
- Ground flaxseed, 2 tbsp ≈ 20 g
- Chopped walnuts, 30 g
- Raisins, 30 g

PREPARATION 10 min:

Peel and dice the apple. Gather all other ingredients.

COOKING 10 min:

In a large bowl, combine the rolled oats, unsweetened applesauce, almond butter, honey, ground cinnamon, vanilla extract, ground flaxseed, chopped walnuts, and raisins. Mix well until everything is thoroughly combined. Add the diced apple to the mixture and fold it in until evenly distributed.

ASSEMBLY 5 min:

Form the mixture into bite-sized balls, about 2.5 cm in diameter. Place the balls on a baking sheet lined with parchment paper.

CHILLING 30 min:

Chill in the refrigerator for at least 30 minutes before serving.

CAL	110 kcal	SODIUM	2 mg
CARBS	17 g	POTASSIUM	130 mg
PROTEIN	3 g	CALCIUM	20 mg
FAT	4 g	MAGNESIUM	25 g

per serving

PEACH YOGURT POPSICLES

6 popsicles | **20 min** | **100 kcal**

- Low-fat plain yogurt, 480 ml
- Fresh peaches, peeled and chopped, 2 medium ≈ 300 g
- Honey, 2 tablespoons ≈ 30 ml
- Lemon juice, 1 tablespoon ≈ 15 ml
- Vanilla extract, 1 teaspoon ≈ 5 ml

PREPARATION 10 min:

In a blender, combine the chopped peaches, honey, lemon juice, and vanilla extract. Blend until smooth. In a large bowl, mix the peach puree with the low-fat plain yogurt until the mixture is well combined.

ASSEMBLY 10 min:

Pour the mixture into popsicle molds and insert sticks. Freeze for at least 4 hours, or until completely frozen.

CAL	100 kcal	SODIUM	35 mg
CARBS	20 g	POTASSIUM	200 mg
PROTEIN	4 g	CALCIUM	100 g
FAT	1 g	MAGNESIUM	15 g

per serving

DRINKS & SMOOTHIES

IN LIFE, MUCH LIKE SMOOTHIES,
YOU GET OUT WHAT
YOU PUT IN

GREEN DETOX SMOOTHIE

2 portions | 17 min | 130 kcal

- Spinach, 60 g
- Kale, 60 g
- Cucumber, 1 medium ≈ 200 g
- Green apple, 1 medium ≈ 180 g
- Avocado, 1/2 medium ≈ 75 g
- Lemon juice, 2 tablespoons ≈ 30 ml
- Fresh ginger, 1 teaspoon ≈ 5 g
- Water, 240 ml

PREPARATION 10 min:

Gather all the ingredients. Wash the spinach, kale, cucumber, and green apple. Peel and chop the cucumber, green apple, and avocado. Peel and grate the ginger.

BLENDING 5 min:

In a blender, combine the spinach, kale, cucumber, green apple, avocado, lemon juice, grated ginger, and water. Blend until smooth and creamy. If the smoothie is too thick, add more water to achieve your desired consistency.

ASSEMBLY 2 min:

Pour the smoothie into glasses and serve immediately.

CAL	130 kcal	SODIUM	30 mg
CARBS	22 g	POTASSIUM	650 mg
PROTEIN	3 g	CALCIUM	90 mg
FAT	5 g	MAGNESIUM	40 g

per serving

BERRY BANANA SMOOTHIE

2 portions | 12 min | 210 kcal

- Fresh or frozen mixed berries (strawberries, blueberries, raspberries), 150 g
- Banana, 1 medium ≈ 120 g
- Fat-free plain yogurt, 240 ml
- Unsweetened almond milk, 240 ml
- Chia seeds, 1 tablespoon ≈ 12 g
- Honey, 1 tbsp ≈ 21 g (optional)

PREPARATION 5 min:

Gather all the ingredients. If using fresh berries, wash them. Peel and slice the banana.

MIXING AND COOKING 5 min:

In a blender, combine the mixed berries, banana, yogurt, almond milk, chia seeds, and honey (if using). Blend until smooth and creamy. If the smoothie is too thick, add more almond milk to reach your desired consistency.

ASSEMBLY 2 min:

Pour the smoothie into glasses and serve immediately.

CAL	180 kcal	SODIUM	90 mg
CARBS	38 g	POTASSIUM	600 mg
PROTEIN	7 g	CALCIUM	250 g
FAT	4 g	MAGNESIUM	40 g

per serving

MANGO LASSI

2 portions | **12 min** | **190 kcal**

- Ripe mango, 1 large ≈ 300 g
- Fat-free plain yogurt, 240 ml
- Unsweetened almond milk, 120 ml
- Honey, 1 tablespoon ≈ 21 g
- Ground cardamom, 1/4 teaspoon
- Ice cubes, 4-5

PREPARATION 5 min:

Gather all the ingredients. Peel and chop the mango.

COOKING 5 min:

In a blender, combine the chopped mango, yogurt, almond milk, honey, ground cardamom, and ice cubes. Blend until smooth and frothy.

ASSEMBLY 2 min:

Pour the lassi into glasses and serve immediately.

CAL	190 kcal	SODIUM	70 mg
CARBS	36 g	POTASSIUM	400 mg
PROTEIN	6 g	CALCIUM	200 g
FAT	2 g	MAGNESIUM	25 g

per serving

ICED GREEN TEA WITH MINT

2 portions | **20 min** | **40 kcal**

- Green tea bags, 2
- Fresh mint leaves, 10 g
- Water, 500 ml
- Honey, 1 tbsp ≈ 21 g (optional)
- Ice cubes, 200 g
- Lemon slices, for garnish

PREPARATION 5 min:

Gather all the ingredients. Rinse the fresh mint leaves.

COOKING 10 min:

Boil 500 ml of water. Once boiling, remove from heat and add the green tea bags and fresh mint leaves. Steep for 5-7 minutes. Remove the tea bags and mint leaves. Stir in the honey (if using) while the tea is still warm. Allow the tea to cool to room temperature.

ASSEMBLY 5 min:

Fill two glasses with ice cubes. Pour the cooled green tea over the ice. Garnish with lemon slices and additional mint leaves if desired. Serve immediately.

CAL	40 kcal	SODIUM	10 mg
CARBS	10 g	POTASSIUM	15 mg
PROTEIN	0 g	CALCIUM	2 g
FAT	0 g	MAGNESIUM	1 g

per serving

CITRUS AND BERRY INFUSED WATER

4 portions — **15 min** — **15 kcal**

- Orange, 1 medium ≈ 130 g
- Lemon, 1 medium ≈ 65 g
- Lime, 1 medium ≈ 70 g
- Fresh strawberries, 100 g
- Fresh blueberries, 50 g
- Fresh raspberries, 50 g
- Fresh mint leaves, 10 g
- Water, 1 liter
- Ice cubes, 200 g

PREPARATION 10 min:

Gather all the ingredients. Wash the fruits and mint leaves. Slice the orange, lemon, and lime. Hull and halve the strawberries.

ASSEMBLY 5 min:

In a large pitcher, combine the sliced orange, lemon, lime, halved strawberries, blueberries, raspberries, and mint leaves. Add 1 liter of water and stir gently. Refrigerate for at least 1 hour to allow the flavors to infuse. Just before serving, add the ice cubes to the pitcher. Pour the infused water into glasses and serve immediately.

CAL	15 kcal	SODIUM	2 mg
CARBS	4 g	POTASSIUM	45 mg
PROTEIN	0 g	CALCIUM	10 mg
FAT	0 g	MAGNESIUM	3 g

per serving

CARROT ORANGE GINGER JUICE

2 portions — **17 min** — **110 kcal**

- Carrots, 300 g
- Oranges, 2 medium ≈ 260 g
- Fresh ginger, 10 g
- Water, 240 ml
- Ice cubes, 200 g

PREPARATION 10 min:

Gather all the ingredients. Wash and peel the carrots, oranges, and ginger. Cut the carrots into smaller pieces. Peel and segment the oranges. Chop the ginger.

COOKING 5 min:

In a blender, combine the carrots, orange segments, chopped ginger, and water. Blend until smooth. Strain the mixture through a fine-mesh sieve or cheesecloth into a pitcher to remove the pulp.

ASSEMBLY 2 min:

Fill two glasses with ice cubes. Pour the juice over the ice. Serve immediately.

CAL	110 kcal	SODIUM	65 mg
CARBS	25 g	POTASSIUM	540 mg
PROTEIN	2 g	CALCIUM	60 g
FAT	0 g	MAGNESIUM	20 g

per serving

PINEAPPLE SPINACH SMOOTHIE

2 portions | 12 min | 190 kcal

- Fresh spinach, 60 g
- Pineapple, 200 g
- Banana, 1 medium ≈ 120 g
- Unsweetened almond milk, 240 ml
- Chia seeds, 1 tablespoon ≈ 12 g
- Fresh ginger, 1 teaspoon ≈ 5 g

PREPARATION 5 min:

Gather all the ingredients. Wash the spinach. Peel and chop the pineapple and banana. Peel and grate the ginger.

COOKING 5 min:

In a blender, combine the spinach, pineapple, banana, almond milk, chia seeds, and grated ginger. Blend until smooth and creamy. If the smoothie is too thick, add more almond milk to reach your desired consistency.

ASSEMBLY 2 min:

Pour the smoothie into glasses and serve immediately.

CAL	190 kcal	SODIUM	80 mg
CARBS	37 g	POTASSIUM	450 mg
PROTEIN	3 g	CALCIUM	170 g
FAT	4 g	MAGNESIUM	50 g

per serving

WATERMELON MINT COOLER

2 portions | 12 min | 70 kcal

- Watermelon, 500 g
- Fresh mint leaves, 10 g
- Lime, 1 medium ≈ 70 g
- Water, 240 ml
- Ice cubes, 200 g

PREPARATION 5 min:

Gather all the ingredients. Cut the watermelon into chunks and remove the seeds. Wash the mint leaves. Juice the lime.

COOKING 5 min:

In a blender, combine the watermelon chunks, mint leaves, lime juice, and water. Blend until smooth. Strain the mixture through a fine-mesh sieve or cheesecloth into a pitcher to remove any pulp.

ASSEMBLY 5 min:

Fill two glasses with ice cubes. Pour the cooler over the ice. Serve immediately.

CAL	70 kcal	SODIUM	5 mg
CARBS	18 g	POTASSIUM	250 mg
PROTEIN	1 g	CALCIUM	20 g
FAT	0 g	MAGNESIUM	15 g

per serving

BEETROOT AND APPLE JUICE

4 portions | **17 min** | **130 kcal**

- Beetroot, 2 medium ≈ 200 g
- Apples, 2 medium ≈ 360 g
- Carrot, 1 medium ≈ 70 g
- Fresh ginger, 10 g
- Water, 240 ml
- Ice cubes, 200 g

PREPARATION 10 min:

Gather all the ingredients. Wash and peel the beetroot, apples, carrot, and ginger. Cut the beetroot, apples, and carrot into smaller pieces. Chop the ginger.

COOKING 5 min:

In a blender, combine the beetroot, apples, carrot, ginger, and water. Blend until smooth. Strain the mixture through a fine-mesh sieve or cheesecloth into a pitcher to remove the pulp.

ASSEMBLY 2 min:

Fill two glasses with ice cubes. Pour the juice over the ice. Serve immediately.

CAL	130 kcal	SODIUM	70 mg
CARBS	31 g	POTASSIUM	250 mg
PROTEIN	2 g	CALCIUM	30 mg
FAT	0 g	MAGNESIUM	25 g

per serving

TROPICAL COCONUT SMOOTHIE

2 portions | **12 min** | **250 kcal**

- Pineapple, 200 g
- Mango, 1 medium ≈ 200 g
- Banana, 1 medium ≈ 120 g
- Unsweetened coconut milk, 240 ml
- Chia seeds, 1 tablespoon ≈ 12 g
- Ice cubes, 200 g

PREPARATION 5 min:

Gather all the ingredients. Peel and chop the pineapple, mango, and banana.

COOKING 5 min:

In a blender, combine the pineapple, mango, banana, coconut milk, and chia seeds. Blend until smooth and creamy. If the smoothie is too thick, add more coconut milk to achieve your desired consistency.

ASSEMBLY 2 min:

Fill two glasses with ice cubes. Pour the smoothie over the ice. Serve immediately.

CAL	250 kcal	SODIUM	35 mg
CARBS	45 g	POTASSIUM	550 mg
PROTEIN	3 g	CALCIUM	45 g
FAT	7 g	MAGNESIUM	40 g

per serving

STRAWBERRY LEMONADE

4 portions | **17 min** | **45 kcal**

- Fresh strawberries, 300 g
- Lemons, 2 medium ≈ 130 g
- Water, 750 ml
- Honey, 2 tbsp ≈ 42 g (optional)
- Ice cubes, 200 g
- Fresh mint leaves, for garnish

PREPARATION 10 min:

Gather all the ingredients. Wash the strawberries and mint leaves. Hull and halve the strawberries. Juice the lemons.

COOKING 5 min:

In a blender, combine the strawberries, lemon juice, water, and honey (if using). Blend until smooth. Strain the mixture through a fine-mesh sieve or cheesecloth into a pitcher to remove the pulp.

ASSEMBLY 2 min:

Fill glasses with ice cubes. Pour the strawberry lemonade over the ice. Garnish with fresh mint leaves. Serve immediately.

CAL	45 kcal	SODIUM	5 mg
CARBS	11 g	POTASSIUM	95 mg
PROTEIN	0 g	CALCIUM	15 g
FAT	0 g	MAGNESIUM	5 g

per serving

CLASSIC LEMONADE

4 portions | **17 min** | **85 kcal**

- Lemons, 4 medium ≈ 260 g
- Water, 1 liter
- Honey, 5 tablespoons ≈ 100 g
- Fresh mint leaves, 10 g
- Ice cubes, 200 g

PREPARATION 10 min:

Gather all the ingredients. Wash the lemons and mint leaves. Juice the lemons.

COOKING 5 min:

In a large pitcher, combine the lemon juice, water, honey, and mint leaves. Stir well until the honey is fully dissolved and the mint leaves are slightly bruised to release their flavor. Let it sit for a few minutes for better infusion.

ASSEMBLY 2 min:

Fill glasses with ice cubes. Pour the lemonade over the ice. Serve immediately.

CAL	85 kcal	SODIUM	5 mg
CARBS	23 g	POTASSIUM	50 mg
PROTEIN	0 g	CALCIUM	10 g
FAT	0 g	MAGNESIUM	3 g

per serving

AVOCADO BANANA SMOOTHIE

2 portions | 12 min | 260 kcal

- Avocado, 1 medium ≈ 150 g
- Banana, 1 medium ≈ 120 g
- Unsweetened almond milk, 240 ml
- Spinach, 30 g
- Chia seeds, 1 tablespoon ≈ 12 g
- Honey, 1 tbsp ≈ 21 g (optional)
- Ice cubes, 200 g

PREPARATION 5 min:

Gather all the ingredients. Wash the spinach. Peel and chop the avocado and banana.

COOKING 5 min:

In a blender, combine the avocado, banana, almond milk, spinach, chia seeds, and honey (if using). Blend until smooth and creamy. If the smoothie is too thick, add more almond milk to achieve your desired consistency.

ASSEMBLY 2 min:

Fill two glasses with ice cubes. Pour the smoothie over the ice. Serve immediately.

CAL	260 kcal	SODIUM	60 mg
CARBS	32 g	POTASSIUM	700 mg
PROTEIN	4 g	CALCIUM	150 mg
FAT	14 g	MAGNESIUM	60 g

per serving

CUCUMBER MINT COOLER

2 portions | 15 min | 70 kcal

- Cucumber, 1 large ≈ 300 g
- Fresh mint leaves, 15 g
- Fresh lime juice, 2 tbsp ≈ 30 ml
- Honey, 1 tablespoon ≈ 15 ml
- Cold water, 500 ml
- Ice cubes, 1 cup ≈ 240 ml

PREPARATION 10 min:

Peel the cucumber and cut it into chunks. Wash the mint leaves thoroughly. In a blender, add the cucumber chunks, mint leaves, lime juice, honey, and cold water. Blend until smooth.

ASSEMBLY 5 min:

Strain the mixture through a fine-mesh sieve into a pitcher to remove any pulp. Pour the strained liquid into glasses filled with ice cubes. Garnish with additional mint leaves if desired.

CAL	70 kcal	SODIUM	5 mg
CARBS	18 g	POTASSIUM	220 mg
PROTEIN	1 g	CALCIUM	30 g
FAT	0 g	MAGNESIUM	15 g

per serving

SAUCES & DRESSINGS

SAUCES ARE THE MAGIC THAT TRANSFORMS ORDINARY DISHES INTO CULINARY MASTERPIECES!

BALSAMIC VINAIGRETTE

6 portions | 10 min | 80 kcal

- Balsamic vinegar, 3 tbsp ≈ 45 ml
- Olive oil, 4 tbsp ≈ 60 ml
- Dijon mustard, 1 tsp ≈ 5 g
- Honey, 1 tsp ≈ 7 g
- Garlic, minced, 1 clove ≈ 3 g
- Black pepper, a pinch
- No salt

PREPARATION 5 min:

Gather all the ingredients. Peel and mince the garlic clove.

MIXING 5 min:

In a small bowl, whisk together the balsamic vinegar, Dijon mustard, honey, and minced garlic until well combined. Slowly add the olive oil while whisking continuously until the dressing is emulsified. Season with a pinch of black pepper and mix well.

BEST FOR:

Balsamic Vinaigrette is ideal for green salads, roasted vegetable salads, and as a marinade for grilled chicken. It adds a rich, tangy flavor that complements a variety of dishes.

CAL	80 kcal	SODIUM	2 mg
CARBS	2 g	POTASSIUM	10 mg
PROTEIN	0,2 g	CALCIUM	2 mg
FAT	8 g	MAGNESIUM	1 g

per serving

TOMATO BASIL SAUCE

2 portions | 12 min | 110 kcal

- Fresh tomatoes, 800 g
- Olive oil, 2 tablespoons ≈ 30 ml
- Garlic, 4 cloves
- Fresh basil leaves, 20 g
- Onion, 1 medium ≈ 150 g
- Carrot, 1 small ≈ 70 g
- Celery stalk, 1 ≈ 50 g
- Dried oregano, 1 teaspoon ≈ 1 g
- Black pepper, 1/2 teaspoon ≈ 1 g
- No salt

PREPARATION 10 min:

Peel and finely chop the garlic. Dice the onion, carrot, and celery. Wash and chop the basil leaves.

COOKING 45 min:

In a large saucepan, heat the olive oil over medium heat. Add garlic, onion, carrot, and celery, and sauté for 10 min until soft. Dice tomatoes and add to the saucepan. Add oregano and black pepper. Stir well. Simmer over low heat for 30 min, stirring occasionally, until thickened. Add basil leaves during the last 5 min of cooking. Use an immersion blender to puree the sauce to your desired consistency, or leave it chunky if preferred.

BEST FOR:

Tomato Basil Sauce is best suited for whole grain pasta, grilled vegetables, and baked fish. It can also be used as a sauce for homemade pizza or baked dishes like chicken Parmesan.

CAL	110 kcal	SODIUM	20 mg
CARBS	14 g	POTASSIUM	480 mg
PROTEIN	2 g	CALCIUM	40 g
FAT	7 g	MAGNESIUM	20 g

per serving

LEMON HERB YOGURT DRESSING

6 portions | **15 min** | **45 kcal**

- Low-fat plain Greek yogurt, 240 ml
- Fresh lemon juice, 2 tbsp ≈ 30 ml
- Lemon zest, 1 tsp ≈ 2 g
- Fresh dill, chopped, 1 tbsp ≈ 3 g
- Fresh parsley, chopped, 1 tbsp ≈ 3 g
- Fresh chives, chopped, 1 tbsp ≈ 3 g
- Olive oil, 1 tbsp ≈ 15 ml
- Garlic, minced, 1 clove ≈ 3 g
- Black pepper, 1/4 tsp ≈ 1 g
- No salt

PREPARATION 10 min:

Gather all ingredients. Finely chop the dill, parsley, and chives, and mince the garlic clove.

MIXING 5 min:

In a medium mixing bowl, combine the Greek yogurt, lemon juice, and lemon zest. Whisk until smooth. Add the chopped herbs, minced garlic, olive oil, and black pepper. Stir well to combine all ingredients thoroughly. Transfer the dressing to a jar or container for storage.

BEST FOR:

Lemon Herb Yogurt Dressing is versatile and pairs well with a variety of dishes. Drizzle over grilled or baked fish for a fresh, tangy flavor. Use as a dipping sauce for vegetable or seafood rolls. Toss with mixed greens, cucumber, and tomatoes for a light, herbaceous salad. Serve as a sauce for grilled or roasted chicken.

CAL	45 kcal	SODIUM	40 mg
CARBS	2 g	POTASSIUM	90 mg
PROTEIN	4 g	CALCIUM	50 g
FAT	3 g	MAGNESIUM	8 g

per serving

LEMON TAHINI DRESSING

8 portions | **15 min** | **70 kcal**

- Tahini, 60 g (≈ 4 tbsp)
- Lemon juice, freshly squeezed, 60 ml (≈ 4 tbsp)
- Water, 60 ml (≈ 4 tbsp)
- Olive oil, 15 ml (≈ 1 tbsp)
- Garlic, minced, 1 clove
- Ground cumin, 1/2 tsp
- Ground black pepper, 1/4 tsp
- No salt

PREPARATION 10 min:

In a medium bowl, whisk together tahini and lemon juice until smooth. Gradually add water while whisking until creamy. Stir in olive oil, minced garlic, ground cumin, and black pepper until fully combined.

ASSEMBLY 5 min:

Taste and adjust seasoning if needed. Transfer dressing to a jar or airtight container for storage.

BEST FOR:

Lemon tahini sauce is perfect for green and vegetable salads, giving them a fresh, creamy flavor. This sauce also pairs excellently with roasted vegetables and works great as a dip for fresh vegetables or whole grain bread.

CAL	70 kcal	SODIUM	10 mg
CARBS	2 g	POTASSIUM	60 mg
PROTEIN	2 g	CALCIUM	20 g
FAT	6 g	MAGNESIUM	10 g

per serving

AVOCADO LIME DRESSING

VG

🍽 4 portions   ⏱ 15 min   🔥 100 kcal

- Avocado, 1 medium ≈ 150 g
- Fresh lime juice, 3 tbsp ≈ 45 ml
- Olive oil, 2 tbsp ≈ 30 ml
- Fresh cilantro, 2 tbsp ≈ 10 g
- Garlic, 1 clove ≈ 3 g
- Water, 3 tbsp ≈ 45 ml
- Black pepper, a pinch
- No salt

PREPARATION 10 min:

Gather all ingredients. Cut avocado in half, remove the pit, and scoop the flesh into a blender. Peel the garlic clove.

BLENDING 5 min:

Add lime juice, olive oil, cilantro, garlic, and water to the blender. Blend until smooth. If too thick, add water, 1 tbsp at a time, until desired consistency. Add a pinch of black pepper and blend again.

BEST FOR:

Avocado Lime Dressing pairs well with mixed green salads, grain bowls, tacos, burritos, veggie wraps, and as a dip for fresh vegetables. It adds a creamy, tangy, and fresh flavor to enhance any dish.

CAL	100 kcal	SODIUM	2 mg
CARBS	4 g	POTASSIUM	250 mg
PROTEIN	1 g	CALCIUM	10 mg
FAT	9 g	MAGNESIUM	15 g

per serving

HONEY MUSTARD DRESSING

VT

🍽 4 portions   ⏱ 10 min   🔥 100 kcal

- Dijon mustard, 2 tbsp ≈ 30 g
- Honey, 2 tbsp ≈ 42 g
- Apple cider vinegar, 2 tbsp ≈ 30 ml
- Olive oil, 2 tbsp ≈ 30 ml
- Water, 1 tbsp ≈ 15 ml
- Black pepper, a pinch
- No salt

PREPARATION 5 min:

Gather all ingredients. Measure out the mustard, honey, vinegar, olive oil, and water.

MIXING 5 min:

In a small bowl, whisk together Dijon mustard and honey until smooth. Gradually add vinegar and olive oil, whisking continuously. Add water to thin the dressing to desired consistency. Season with a pinch of black pepper and mix well.

BEST FOR:

Honey Mustard Dressing is perfect for green salads, chicken salads, and as a dip for roasted vegetables or chicken tenders. It adds a sweet and tangy flavor that enhances the taste of various dishes.

CAL	100 kcal	SODIUM	40 mg
CARBS	9 g	POTASSIUM	15 mg
PROTEIN	0,5 g	CALCIUM	10 g
FAT	7 g	MAGNESIUM	5 g

per serving

SMOKY CHIPOTLE YOGURT SAUCE

6 servings | 15 min | 50 kcal

- Low-fat plain Greek yogurt, 240 ml
- Chipotle peppers in adobo sauce, 2 tbsp ≈ 30 g
- Fresh lime juice, 1 tbsp ≈ 15 ml
- Honey, 1 tsp ≈ 7 g
- Garlic powder, 1/2 tsp ≈ 2 g
- Smoked paprika, 1/2 tsp ≈ 2 g
- Cumin powder, 1/4 tsp ≈ 1 g
- Black pepper, 1/4 tsp ≈ 1 g
- A pinch of salt

PREPARATION 10 min:

Gather all ingredients. Finely chop the chipotle peppers.

MIXING 5 min:

In a medium mixing bowl, combine the Greek yogurt, chopped chipotle peppers, lime juice, honey, garlic powder, smoked paprika, cumin powder, black pepper, and a pinch of salt. Stir well to combine all ingredients thoroughly until smooth and creamy. Transfer the sauce to a jar or container for storage.

BEST FOR:

Smoky Chipotle Yogurt Sauce is perfect for adding a smoky, spicy kick to a variety of dishes. Use it as a topping for tacos and burritos, or drizzle it over grilled vegetables or meats for extra flavor.

CAL	50 kcal	SODIUM	60 mg
CARBS	3 g	POTASSIUM	100 mg
PROTEIN	4 g	CALCIUM	50 g
FAT	2 g	MAGNESIUM	8 g

per serving

CILANTRO LIME DRESSING

4 portions | 15 min | 90 kcal

- Fresh cilantro, 1 cup ≈ 30 g
- Fresh lime juice, 3 tbsp ≈ 45 ml
- Olive oil, 1/4 cup ≈ 60 ml
- Greek yogurt, low-fat, 1/2 cup ≈ 120 g
- Garlic, minced, 1 clove ≈ 3 g
- Honey, 1 tsp ≈ 7 g
- Water, 2 tbsp ≈ 30 ml
- Black pepper, a pinch

PREPARATION 10 min:

Gather all the ingredients. Chop the cilantro, and peel and mince the garlic clove.

BLENDING 5 min:

In a blender or food processor, combine cilantro, lime juice, olive oil, Greek yogurt, minced garlic, honey, and water. Blend until the ingredients are well mixed but still slightly chunky. Add a pinch of black pepper and blend briefly again to mix.

BEST FOR:

Cilantro Lime Dressing is perfect for green salads, taco salads, and grilled chicken or fish. It adds a bright, tangy flavor that enhances many dishes.

CAL	90 kcal	SODIUM	5 mg
CARBS	3 g	POTASSIUM	100 mg
PROTEIN	2 g	CALCIUM	40 g
FAT	8 g	MAGNESIUM	5 g

per serving

SPICY PEANUT SAUCE

4 portions | 15 min | 120 kcal

- Natural peanut butter, 1/4 cup ≈ 64 g
- Low-sodium soy sauce, 2 tbsp
- Fresh lime juice, 1 tbsp ≈ 15 ml
- Honey, 1 tbsp ≈ 21 g
- Sriracha sauce, 1 tsp ≈ 5
- Fresh ginger, 1 tsp ≈ 5 g
- Garlic, minced, 1 clove ≈ 3 g
- Water, 2 tbsp ≈ 30 ml (optional)
- Black pepper, a pinch

PREPARATION 10 min:

Gather all the ingredients. Grate the fresh ginger and mince the garlic clove.

MIXING 5 min:

In a medium bowl, combine peanut butter, soy sauce, lime juice, honey, Sriracha sauce, ginger, and garlic. Mix until well combined but slightly chunky, as shown in the image. If too thick, add water, 1 tbsp at a time, until desired consistency. Season with a pinch of black pepper and stir again.

BEST FOR:

Spicy Peanut Sauce is perfect for whole grain noodle dishes and as a dip for spring rolls or grilled chicken skewers. It adds a rich, spicy, and nutty flavor that enhances a variety of Asian-inspired dishes.

CAL	120 kcal	SODIUM	150 mg
CARBS	7 g	POTASSIUM	100 mg
PROTEIN	4 g	CALCIUM	10 mg
FAT	9 g	MAGNESIUM	20 g

per serving

ROASTED RED PEPPER SAUCE

4 portions | 45 min | 70 kcal

- Red bell peppers, 2 large ≈ 300 g
- Olive oil, 2 tbsp ≈ 30 ml
- Garlic, minced, 2 cloves ≈ 6 g
- Fresh lemon juice, 1 tbsp ≈ 15 ml
- Fresh basil, 2 tbsp ≈ 10 g
- Greek yogurt, low-fat, 1/4 cup ≈ 60 g
- Black pepper, a pinch
- No salt

PREPARATION 15 min:

Gather all the ingredients. Preheat oven to 220°C (425°F). Cut bell peppers in half, remove seeds and stems.

ROASTING 20 min:

Place bell pepper halves on a baking sheet, cut side down. Drizzle with 1 tbsp olive oil. Roast for about 20 minutes until skins are blistered and charred. Remove and let cool.

BLENDING 10 min:

Peel the skins off the roasted peppers. In a blender, combine pepper flesh, minced garlic, lemon juice, basil, Greek yogurt, remaining olive oil, and black pepper. Blend until smooth but slightly chunky, as shown in the image.

BEST FOR:

Roasted Red Pepper Sauce is perfect for pasta dishes, grain bowls, and as a topping for grilled chicken or fish. It adds a rich, smoky, and slightly sweet flavor that enhances a variety of dishes.

CAL	70 kcal	SODIUM	10 mg
CARBS	5 g	POTASSIUM	200 mg
PROTEIN	2 g	CALCIUM	20 g
FAT	5 g	MAGNESIUM	10 g

per serving

TABLE OF INGREDIENT SUBSTITUTIONS

Healthy eating is essential for feeling good and staying energetic throughout the day. All the recipes in this book follow the principles of healthy eating and the DASH diet. However, many recipes you might find online or on YouTube contain ingredients that don't always meet these standards. The table below provides healthy alternatives to popular but less nutritious ingredients. These substitutions will help you experiment with recipes while adhering to the DASH diet and maintaining a healthy lifestyle.

Ingredient to Replace	Substitute	Benefits of Substitution
Salt	Lemon juice, herbs (basil, oregano), garlic, onion, black pepper, ginger	Reduces sodium intake, enhances flavor
Butter	Avocado, Greek yogurt, applesauce, coconut oil	Reduces saturated fats, adds additional nutrients
Sugar	Honey, stevia, maple syrup, agave syrup, fruit puree (banana, apple)	Reduces calories, lower glycemic index
White flour	Whole wheat flour, almond flour, coconut flour, oats	Increases fiber, vitamins, and minerals
Sour cream	Greek yogurt, low-fat cream cheese, coconut yogurt	Reduces calories and fats, adds additional protein
Mayonnaise	Avocado, yogurt sauce, mustard, hummus	Reduces saturated fats, increases healthy fats
Whole milk	Skim milk, almond milk, soy milk, coconut milk	Reduces saturated fats, adds additional nutrients
White rice	Brown rice, quinoa, bulgur, whole grain couscous, riced cauliflower	Increases fiber, protein, vitamins, and minerals
Red meat	Chicken, turkey, fish, tofu, tempeh, legumes	Reduces saturated fats, increases protein and healthy fats
Full-fat cheese	Low-fat cheese, feta cheese, tofu, nutritional yeast	Reduces saturated fats and calories, adds additional protein
Sugary drinks	Water with lemon, herbal teas, coconut water, unsweetened sparkling water	Reduces sugar and calorie intake
Mashed potatoes	Mashed cauliflower, sweet potatoes, pumpkin	Increases fiber, reduces calories
White bread	Whole grain bread, seeded bread, gluten-free bread	Increases fiber, vitamins, and minerals
Coffee cream	Skim milk, almond milk, coconut milk	Reduces saturated fats and calories
Regular pasta	Whole grain pasta, chickpea pasta, lentil pasta, zucchini noodles	Increases protein and fiber, reduces calories
Ketchup	Homemade tomato sauce, tomato paste, avocado puree	Reduces sugar and sodium intake

Use this table to make your dishes lower in calories, reduce the amount of saturated fats and sodium, and increase the amount of beneficial nutrients.

YOUR NEXT STEPS

As we conclude this book, I want to emphasize that your health is in your hands. The DASH diet is not just a temporary solution but a lifestyle that can help you achieve long-term results.

Continue learning about the DASH diet and healthy eating in general. The more you know, the easier it will be to make informed choices. Experiment with recipes, discover new favorite dishes, and enjoy the process. Don't be afraid to adapt your diet to your needs, but always remember the basics and main principles briefly described in this book. Plan your meals and monitor your well-being to understand how changes in your diet affect your body.

Your goal is to create a balanced diet that you enjoy and that benefits you.

Find support by connecting with others who are also following the DASH diet. Join online communities, local groups, or find a friend to share the journey with. Remember, sustainable change takes time. Be patient with yourself and celebrate the small victories along the way. Every step you take towards health is significant. No matter where you are in your journey, keep moving forward. Let this book be your faithful companion and source of inspiration.

Printed in Great Britain
by Amazon